JUSTIFYING WAR

Richard Norton-Taylor

JUSTIFYING WAR

Scenes from the Hutton Inquiry

OBERON BOOKS
LONDON

First published in 2003 by Oberon Books Ltd.
(incorporating Absolute Classics)
521 Caledonian Road, London N7 9RH
Tel: 020 7607 3637 / Fax: 020 7607 3629
e-mail: oberon.books@btinternet.com

A catalogue record for this book is available from the British Library.

ISBN: 1 84002 417 8

Cover design: Graham Caws Graphic Design

Printed in Great Britain by Antony Rowe Ltd, Chippenham.

Characters

THE RIGHT HONOURABLE LORD HUTTON

<u>THE LAWYERS</u>
JAMES DINGEMANS QC
PETER KNOX

<u>THE WITNESSES</u>
PATRICK LAMB
ANDREW GILLIGAN
SUSAN WATTS
MARTIN HOWARD
ALASTAIR CAMPBELL
JAMES BLITZ
ANDREW MACKINLAY MP
GEOFF HOON MP
WING COMMANDER JOHN CLARK
GAVYN DAVIES
DR BRIAN JONES
MRS JANICE KELLY

Justifying War was first performed at The Tricycle Theatre, London on 30 October 2003, with the following cast:

THE RIGHT HONOURABLE LORD HUTTON,
James Woolley

THE LAWYERS

JAMES DINGEMANS QC, Mark Penfold

PETER KNOX, Adam Barker

THE WITNESSES

PATRICK LAMB, Thomas Wheatley

ANDREW GILLIGAN, William Chubb

SUSAN WATTS, Sally Giles

MARTIN HOWARD, David Beames

ALASTAIR CAMPBELL, David Michaels

JAMES BLITZ, Thomas Wheatley

ANDREW MACKINLAY MP, Roland Oliver

GEOFF HOON MP, Kenneth Bryans

WING COMMANDER JOHN CLARK, David Beames

GAVYN DAVIES, David Fleeshman

DR BRIAN JONES, William Hoyland

MRS JANICE KELLY, Sally Giles

Director, Nicolas Kent with Charlotte Westenra
Designer, Claire Spooner
Lighting, Johanna Town
Sound, Shaz McGee & Mike Thacker

Producer's Note

Lord Hutton's Inquiry into the circumstances surrounding the death of Dr David Kelly sat for 25 days and heard from 75 witnesses. These edited transcripts are taken from the evidence of 12 witnesses in the first part of the Inquiry.

The evidence is presented chronologically, with the exception of that of Dr Jones. He gave his evidence two days after Mrs Kelly. It is presented here before her evidence. Of the witnesses we have chosen, all but five (Watts, Blitz, Mackinlay, Mrs Kelly and Dr Jones) were recalled for cross-examination in part 2 of the Inquiry.

The main purpose of the second part was to allow the earlier evidence to be tested in cross-examination by opposing counsel representing the Government – both ministers and officials – Dr Kelly's family, and the BBC and to be questioned further by counsel for the Inquiry itself.

Lord Hutton is expected to present his report to the Government in the New Year.

The text in square brackets indicates an addition [made for clarification purposes] to the original hearing script.

The following text was correct at the time of going to press.

USHER: Ladies and gentleman, could you please switch off your mobile phones.

Silence. All rise.

Opening Statement by Lord Hutton, 1st August 2003

HUTTON: This Inquiry relates to a very tragic death. Therefore, ladies and gentlemen, I think it would be fitting if we stood for a minute's silence in memory of Dr Kelly. My terms of reference are these: 'Urgently to conduct an investigation into the circumstances surrounding the death of Dr Kelly.' First of all, my primary task is to investigate the circumstances surrounding the death and that will involve a detailed and careful examination of the relevant facts. Secondly, my terms of reference require me to conduct the investigation urgently, and that means I must proceed with expedition. Thirdly, I must ensure that the procedures at the Inquiry are fair to those who give evidence. It is also important that I should emphasise that this is an Inquiry to be conducted by me – it is not a trial conducted between interested parties who have conflicting cases to advance. I do not sit to decide between conflicting cases – I sit to investigate the circumstances surrounding Dr Kelly's death.

Patrick Lamb, 11th August 2003

DINGEMANS: While we are waiting we might as well get have DOS 1/55. Mr Lamb, could you tell his Lordship your full name?

LAMB: My full name is Patrick Lamb.

DINGEMANS: And what is your current occupation?

LAMB: I am presently the deputy head of the Counter Proliferation Department in the Foreign and

Commonwealth Office. I worked very closely with David Kelly.

DINGEMANS: Can I deal with the dossier. Now I think you have disclosed that Dr Kelly was involved in April 2002 in the first draft.

LAMB: Correct.

DINGEMANS: Was he involved in the May additions?

LAMB: Yes, he was. At all times we would show the text to David and we would very much rely on his expertise and knowledge, as the source and person who could verify the accuracy of what we were producing.

DINGEMANS: That was because of his involvement in the UNSCOM inspections?

LAMB: Very much so. He obviously had direct involvement. Often, I can recall, if I had to make a choice between a textual choice and Dr Kelly, I would often back Dr Kelly ahead of the textual source

DINGEMANS: But it appears that David Kelly had further involvement, is that right?

LAMB: He had further involvement through me, which is that after the decision by the Prime Minister on 3rd September that there would be a public dossier there was obviously a revision of the constituent parts. Our relationship with Dr Kelly was a very easy one, a very relaxed one; and when he came into the department we would, as a matter of course show him drafts if drafts were available and we would discuss them with him. This was, as I say, on an informal basis.

DINGEMANS: Looking at the contents page [of the dossier], those bits of the chapter that you, in the Foreign and Commonwealth Office, would have discussed, if I can use that term, I hope fairly, with Dr Kelly would be part 2, History of UN Weapons Inspection and chapter 3, The Current Position; is that right?

LAMB: That would be correct. I would add, however, there is also part 3, Iraq Under Saddam Hussein, which became known, informally at least, to those of us involved in the Cabinet Office meetings, as the human rights element of the dossier. There we would have discussed that also with Dr Kelly.

HUTTON: Can I just ask you Mr Lamb on part 2 of the September dossier Dr Kelly would have commented on that, he did not actually write it, he commented on it, but he actually wrote, did he, the first draft of the box on page 38?

LAMB: He would have written what eventually became the first draft in the box on page 38. He also contributed in particular on pages 11 and 12 that relate to the chemical weapons and biological weapons agents developed by Iraq, their lethality and so on; and obviously he acted as technical adviser in that respect.

HUTTON: Yes; but when you say 'contributed', do you mean that he made comments on a draft that you or someone else had written or that he wrote it himself?

LAMB: With respect to Iraq's biological weapons programme, he wrote that himself.

HUTTON: I see, yes. Thank you very much.

DINGEMANS: Is that all that you can help with on the drafting of the dossier, from your point of view?

LAMB: I believe that it is, sir, yes. We worked extremely well in a very happy manner in many respects. It was not a labour of love, it was something we thought was extremely important, continue to believe to be extremely important. I am only very saddened that that happy atmosphere has the shadow of Dr Kelly's death hanging over it.

Andrew Gilligan, 12th August 2003

DINGEMANS: Can you tell his Lordship your full name?

GILLIGAN: Yes, it is Andrew Paul Gilligan. I am the defence and diplomatic correspondent of the Today Programme on Radio 4.

DINGEMANS: Can you tell us when you first met Dr Kelly?

GILLIGAN: Yes, it was in the early months of 2001. I cannot tell you exactly when because I have lost my appointments diary for that year but it was probably in January or February. I was going to Iraq and I wanted to speak to him to discuss, you know, Iraqi related issues with him.

DINGEMANS: How had you come on his name?

GILLIGAN: He had been initially recommended to me by a colleague at the BBC, and I had then found his details in fact in our central contacts database. There is a sort of potted biography of him and it starts by saying: 'If David Kelly were a tax inspector he would recoup Britain's entire national debt.'

DINGEMANS: Did he describe his role in the dossier?

GILLIGAN: He did in outline terms. I said something like: what was your involvement? He said it was to advise on all claims relating to his expertise in the dossier.

DINGEMANS: And what did you understand his expertise to be?

GILLIGAN: Chemical and biological weapons. He had spent a great deal of time in Iraq. He was pretty close to the subject.

DINGEMANS: What view did he convey to you of the Iraqi regime?

GILLIGAN: He was extremely suspicious of them; and I mean he had been involved in many confrontations with them when he was an UNSCOM inspector.

DINGEMANS: Who was responsible for the meeting on 22nd May? Did you contact him or did he contact you?

GILLIGAN: No, I contacted him.

DINGEMANS: Can I take you to diary entry BBC/7/55? You have written 4 o'clock. Did you actually meet at 4 o'clock or could it have been afterwards?

GILLIGAN: I was slightly, you know, maybe 10 or 15 minutes late. He was waiting when I got there.

DINGEMANS: I think you have seen his evidence where he said the meeting was at 5. Does that accord with your recollection?

GILLIGAN: No, I think it was at 4. It was certainly fixed for 4 and then I went on to something else; and I am pretty sure, you know, it would not have started later than about 4.10 or 4.15. I have a drinks receipt, I bought drinks for us.

DINGEMANS: We will come to that. Can we turn to BBC/7/56. You did not have something to eat [at] this time?

GILLIGAN: I do not think so. We might have had some sandwiches or more drinks but that is the only thing I can find.

DINGEMANS: That shows a bottle of Coke and a bottle of Appletize. Can you help me with the time on that?

GILLIGAN: That says 4.15, 16.15. That is the time I went to the bar to buy the drinks.

DINGEMANS: You still have this receipt because I imagine you put this through the BBC accounts, do you?

GILLIGAN: Yes, I need to claim it back for expenses.

DINGEMANS: The notes you made on 22nd May 2003, were those made with a pen and pencil or with some other means?

GILLIGAN: They were made on my personal organiser.

DINGEMANS: Can we turn to BBC/7/57? This is the printout from your personal organiser?

GILLIGAN: Yes.

DINGEMANS: Yes, just reading the note through, if that is alright.

GILLIGAN: 'Transformed week before publication to make it sexier. The classic was the 45 minutes. Most things in dossier were double source but that was single source. Most people in intelligence weren't happy with it because it didn't reflect the considered view they were putting forward. 'Campbell: real information but unreliable, included against our wishes. Not in original draft – dull, he asked if anything else could go in. 'It was small…', this is the programme, I think. 'It was small because you could not conceal a large programme.' I cannot read it, the type is a bit faint.

HUTTON: It looks like 'thin'. Is it 'I think'?

GILLIGAN: 'I think it is 30 per cent likely that Iraq had an active chemical warfare programme?

HUTTON: Is it 'chemical warfare' or 'chemical weapons'?

GILLIGAN: Either really. We started by talking about other things and then we got on to the dossier; and I said: What happened to it? When we last met you were saying it was not very exciting. He said: 'It was transformed in the week before publication'. I said: To make it sexier? And he said: Yes, to make it sexier. Then I said: What do you mean? Can you give me some examples? And he said the classic – he did not use the word example, he said the classic was the 45 minutes, the statement that WMD could be ready in 45 minutes.

DINGEMANS: Then there is the entry which is just a single word, 'Campbell'. Was there any question that gave rise to that entry?

GILLIGAN: Yes, it was something like: how did this transformation happen?

DINGEMANS: Right.

GILLIGAN: And then the answer was that, one word.

DINGEMANS: He said just 'Campbell'?

GILLIGAN: Yes.

DINGEMANS: And what question led to the next entry?

GILLIGAN: Well I was surprised and I said: What, you know, Campbell made it up? They made it up? And he said: No, it was real information but it was unreliable and it was in the dossier against our wishes.

HUTTON: May I just ask you, Mr Gilligan, looking at the first paragraph, you put the question: Was it to make it sexier? And Dr Kelly replied: Yes, to make it sexier?

GILLIGAN: Yes, to make it sexier, yes, so he adopted my words.

HUTTON: Now are you clear in your recollection that you asked how was it transformed, and that the name Campbell was first spoken by Dr Kelly?

GILLIGAN: Yes, absolutely.

HUTTON: It was not a question by you: was Campbell involved in this?

GILLIGAN: No, it was him. He raised the subject of the 45 minutes and he raised the subject of Campbell.

HUTTON: Yes

DINGEMANS: Was there anything else that you did to confirm or deny the story?

GILLIGAN: Well, I went to look at the dossier itself, and to sort of do a sort of textual analysis of the dossier itself.

DINGEMANS: Is there any passages you would like to refer us to?

GILLIGAN: There is a passage on page 18.

DINGEMANS: Page 18 of the dossier, DOS/1/73.

GILLIGAN: This is the right page. It starts off by saying: 'In mid-2001 the Joint Intelligence Committee assessed that Iraq retained some chemical warfare agents from before the Gulf War. These stocks would enable Iraq to produce significant quantities of mustard gas within weeks and of nerve agent within months.' 'Would enable Iraq to produce'. Then you go down to paragraph 8, this is on the next page, on page 19.

DINGEMANS: DOS/1/74.

GILLIGAN: Then you see standing almost on its own a very bald statement: Intelligence 'shows… Iraq has continued to produce chemical agent.' That is not what the earlier bit says. It says it could produce it within weeks. This says it has continued to produce it. There is a paragraph about 'Recent Intelligence' somewhere.

DINGEMANS: The paragraph headed 'Recent Intelligence' is paragraph 5 on DOS/1/73.

GILLIGAN: If you look at what they say the recent intelligence consists of, there is no recent intelligence about production capabilities. So there are inconsistencies in this document; and in all cases it was the harder – the firmer statement, that they actually had weapons rather than just the ability to produce weapons. Those are the statements that make it into the executive summary, into the Prime Minister's foreword.

DINGEMANS: Was there anything else you did?

GILLIGAN: I knew already that the Government had embellished another dossier. They published a dossier in

February 2003 on Iraq's infrastructure of concealment, deception and intimidation. The Prime Minister described it as further intelligence. A good part of it anyway was copied off the Internet. It was copied almost word for word, including the spelling mistakes actually in some cases, but one of the figures was embellished, and a couple of the claims, some of the language was embellished. In the student's original PhD thesis, the wording –

DINGEMANS: What student are you referring to?

GILLIGAN: This is Ibrahim al Marishi. He wrote the thesis which was then copied without acknowledgment. Marishi wrote the Iraqi Mukhabarat had a role in aiding opposition groups in hostile regimes, and that was changed in the February dossier to supporting terrorist organisations in hostile regimes, which is quite a substantial change.

DINGEMANS: Can we then turn to the broadcast itself on the [29th May]? Do you have the second broadcast? Can we look at BBC/1/5? Slightly less dramatically, could you be Andrew Gilligan at the bottom and I will be Mr Humphreys. If we pick it up halfway down the page: '[John] Humphreys: 28 minutes to 8. Tony Blair had quite a job persuading the country and indeed his own MPs to support the invasion of Iraq; his main argument was that Saddam had weapons of mass destruction that threatened us all. None of those weapons has been found. Now our defence correspondent, Andrew Gilligan, has found evidence that the government's dossier on Iraq that was produced last September was cobbled together at the last minute with some unconfirmed material that had not been approved by the Security Services. Are you suggesting, let's be very clear about this, that it was not the work of the intelligence agencies?'

GILLIGAN: No, the information which I'm told was dubious did come from the agencies, but they were unhappy about it, because they didn't think it should have been in there. They thought it was – it was not corroborated sufficiently, and they actually thought it was wrong.

DINGEMANS: At the top of page 6 you continue.

GILLIGAN: I mean let's go through this. This is the dossier that was published in September last year, probably the most substantial statement of the government's case against Iraq. The first thing you see is a preface written by Tony Blair. Tony Blair's words were voiced up by somebody on the production team. Those words were: 'Saddam's military planning allows for some weapons of mass destruction to be ready within forty five minutes of an order to deploy them.' Then it is back to me again: 'Now that claim has come back to haunt Mr Blair because if the weapons had been that readily to hand, they probably would have been found by now. But you know, it could have been an honest mistake, but what I have been told is that the Government knew that claim was questionable even before they wrote it in their dossier. 'I have spoken to a British official who was involved in the preparation of the dossier, and he told me that until the week before it was published, the draft dossier produced by the Intelligence Services, added little to what was already publicly known. He said…' Again, this is a voice up. 'It was transformed in the week before it was published, to make it sexier.'

DINGEMANS: Can we go back to BBC/1/4, which is the transcript for your first broadcast which I think took place shortly after 6 in the morning [of the same day] is that right?

GILLIGAN: Yes, this was at 6.07.

DINGEMANS: Was this contribution to the programme scripted?

GILLIGAN: No, it was not.

DINGEMANS: So this was you speaking from the studio or from home?

GILLIGAN: From home. This is me speaking live and unscripted.

DINGEMANS: Can I take you to this: [You say] '...and what we've been told by one of the senior officials in charge of drawing up that dossier was that actually the Government probably, erm, knew that that forty-five minute figure was wrong, even before it decided to put it in.' Now, we have all been through the note you say you made of Dr Kelly's meeting; this does not appear to be in that note.

GILLIGAN: No. This is not intended to be a direct quote from David Kelly. We were trying to convey the essence of what the source had said.

DINGEMANS: So it was not a direct quotation from the source and you did not portray it as a direct quotation. Was it supported by what Dr Kelly had told you?

GILLIGAN: I believe so.

DINGEMANS: If it was not entirely supported by what Dr Kelly had said, why did you not go back and check it with him?

GILLIGAN: As I say, what this was was a product of a live broadcast. It was, I do believe, a fair conclusion to draw from what he said to me. But I think, on reflection, I did not use exactly the right language. It was not wrong, but it was not perfect either.

DINGEMANS: Was this allegation ever withdrawn at any time before Dr Kelly died?

GILLIGAN: Well, I never returned to the form of words I used in the 6.07 broadcast. Subsequent broadcasts were scripted. The word I used in the 7.32 broadcast, the scripted one, was 'questionable', which I was happier with.

DINGEMANS: Can I then turn to [the Foreign Affairs Committee] FAC/1/94? Can I take you to the final passage, Mr Hamilton['s question]: 'Did you say anything which Mr Gilligan might reasonably have interpreted as identifying Mr Alastair Campbell as wanting to change the dossier or 'sex it up' in any way or make undue reference to the 45 minute claim?' Dr Kelly [says]: 'I cannot recall that. I find it very difficult to think back to a conversation I had six weeks ago. I cannot recall but that does not mean to say, of course, that such a statement was not made but I really cannot recall it. It does not sound like the sort of thing I would say.'

GILLIGAN: I noted that that was not a denial in some respects. I mean, you know 'I cannot recall but that does not mean to say, of course, that such a statement was not made'.

DINGEMANS: Can I take you on to your publication in *The Mail on Sunday* which was BBC/1/27? Why did you name Alastair Campbell in The *Mail on Sunday* piece when you had not on the BBC piece?

GILLIGAN: I had had a difficult relationship with Mr Campbell during the Iraq war. He complained about my coverage several times; and I thought he had a particular issue about some of my reporting. I did not want to be the first to name him in this context. But some of that press follow up did name Mr Campbell in this context, so I thought: well, I am not the first.

DINGEMANS: Can I take you to another complaint that Mr Campbell had made about your reporting in the war. BBC/4/146. This is a letter of 1st April 2003 that Mr Campbell writes to [the BBC Director of News, Richard] Sambrook: Dear Richard, Andrew Gilligan claimed on Radio Five that 'people here are saying the Republican Guard hasn't really been damaged at all and they could be right. Who told him the Republican Guard hasn't been damaged – the Iraqi Ministry of Information? Was this report monitored? Does Mr Gilligan have a minder? Then there are a couple more. Can I take you to the reply at 148? Sorry, at 148 there is another letter from Mr Kaufman making a similar complaint effectively.

GILLIGAN: It is, in fact, identical language, the words are identical.

DINGEMANS: Yes. Then page 149: 'Dear Richard, On Radio 4 this morning, Andrew Gilligan said: 'I'm not quite sure where these intelligence assessments come from. It might just be more rubbish from Central Command.' Do you believe that final sentence was justified? That, as I understand it, was a reference to American central command, is that right?

GILLIGAN: Yes.

DINGEMANS: Then page 150, the response by Mr Sambrook of 2nd April: 'Dear Alastair, Thank you for your letter. Gerald Kaufman has written in strikingly similar terms.'

DINGEMANS: The only purpose of taking you to that correspondence is to show you what I think you have already disclosed, that even if it was not a personal relationship with Alastair Campbell as a professional relationship it was pretty frosty?

GILLIGAN: These are good examples of the kind of relationship that Alastair Campbell has; and it is a good example of the reason why I was reluctant to be the first to name him in the context of transforming the dossier.

DINGEMANS: Can I take you to CAB/1/352. This is the letter dated 26th June 2003 from Alastair Campbell to Mr Sambrook. Can I take you to page 353, where he asked this question : 'Does the BBC still stand by the allegation it made on 29th May that Number Ten added in the 45-minute claim to the dossier? Yes or no? Does it still stand by the allegation made on that day that both we and the intelligence agencies knew the 45 minute claim to be wrong and inserted it despite knowing that? Yes or no?' I think you accepted that your appearance at 6.07 was unscripted, that the language was, I am afraid I do not have the transcript in front of me but not exact?

GILLIGAN: Was not perfect, I think I said.

HUTTON: But you had made the allegation, it was you who had said this on the programme.

GILLIGAN: As I said, the wording in that first two-way was not a fair reflection of how the whole story was covered either by me or by the BBC; and I had repeatedly said, in subsequent broadcasts, that nobody was accusing Downing Street of lying, nobody was accusing Downing Street of making the intelligence – of making the 45 minutes claim up. We made it clear on repeated occasions that it was real intelligence. So if a misleading impression was given and it was given unintentionally, it already had been corrected.

DINGEMANS: You are an experienced reporter - did you think that Dr Kelly would have had the faintest idea what he was letting himself in for?

GILLIGAN: I mean, I think he was pretty experienced at dealing with journalists; I cannot speculate on what Dr Kelly may have felt but he was experienced with journalists.

Susan Watts, 12th and 13th August 2003

WATTS: My full name is Susan Janet Watts and I am a BBC reporter.

HUTTON: Yes. Thank you.

DINGEMANS: What programme do you work with?

WATTS: I work with BBC Newsnight. I am the science editor.

DINGEMANS: Biological and chemical warfare was something you covered?

WATTS: Yes.

DINGEMANS: And in the course of that, on a professional basis, did you come across Dr David Kelly?

WATTS: Yes, I did.

DINGEMANS: How had you got into contact with him?

WATTS: I was given his name by a Foreign Office official.

HUTTON: The Foreign Office gave you Dr Kelly's telephone number.

WATTS: Yes.

DINGEMANS: Your conversations with him, were they all on the same basis, attributable or non-attributable?

WATTS: They were all non-attributable – the information was to be used but not identified as having come from him.

DINGEMANS: Did you have a conversation in April 2003?

WATTS: Yes, we did. We had quite a long telephone conversation. During that conversation he mentioned having had lunch with Geoff Hoon, the Defence Secretary.

DINGEMANS: Did he say what he had talked about at lunch?

WATTS: Well, yes. He talked about – he and I were talking about the process of the search for WMD and Whitehall's attitude to the fact that nothing of significance had been found by then; and Dr Kelly said that Mr Hoon had said to him, rather cryptically Dr Kelly implied, and I quote – Geoff Hoon said to Dr Kelly, 'One sees the mosaic of evidence being built up'.

DINGEMANS: What did you understand Dr Kelly to understand by that rather cryptic comment?

WATTS: Very little in fact. He chuckled about the fact that it was fairly meaningless.

DINGEMANS: What else did Dr Kelly say on that occasion?

WATTS: He expressed a firm wish to return to Iraq and some frustration at not having been asked to go back yet. He talked about the fact that he felt perhaps the security – there was not sufficient security for him to return. During the same conversation we discussed the uranium Niger intelligence issue and my shorthand notes show that he said, and I am quoting, 'That obviously was an improper analysis'.

DINGEMANS: Did you form any view about his access to Government information?

WATTS: Well, from the variety and breadth of it, I formed the view very definitely he had extraordinary access to Government information across the board.

DINGEMANS: Did he tell you in terms what access he had?

WATTS: Not specifically, no. Again, I would say that he was passing information to me that was not sensitive in any way, not operational information.

DINGEMANS: It was not anything that was going to compromise anyone's safety?

WATTS: No, and not whistle-blowing in any sense.

DINGEMANS: Do you have any notes of any other contacts to him?

WATTS: 7th, 12th and 30th of May.

DINGEMANS: Can we go back to the 7th May?

WATTS: Hmm, hmm.

DINGEMANS: Can you, first of all, tell us who initiated the contact?

WATTS: I did I rang him at home, I think, and probably from my home.

DINGEMANS: Did you discuss anything in particular, any development in Iraq?

WATTS: Well, we talked about the most recent developments; and Dr Kelly's view that the process of looking for weapons of mass destruction would likely be a lengthy one unless the teams were to 'strike it lucky'.

DINGEMANS: What was your understanding of Dr Kelly's views about the prospects of finding weapons of mass destruction.

WATTS: My impression is that he very definitely thought that there were weapons programmes. It might well be a lengthy search to find that evidence and it would be a process of pulling together many, many bits of information and that that process is really only beginning.

DINGEMANS: Did you discuss the 45 minutes claim in the Government dossier?

WATTS: Towards the end of the conversation we did, yes.

DINGEMANS: And what did he say about that?

WATTS: Dr Kelly said to me that it was, and I quote: 'A mistake to put in Alastair Campbell seeing something in there, single source but not corroborated, sounded good.'

DINGEMANS: Right. And what was the nature of the way in which he imparted this information? Was it as if this was a revelation or this was a chatty aside?

WATTS: Certainly not a revelation at all, I would characterise as a gossipy aside comment.

DINGEMANS: When Dr Kelly discussed with you the 45 minutes claim, did he discuss any weapons that might have been used to launch chemical and biological weapons?

WATTS: Yes. We talked a bit about why such a precise timing might be used, 45 minutes rather than 43 or 40. He said that he was – he made clear that he, in his word, was guessing; but he said that in 1991 the Iraqis were, and I quote, 'playing around with multibarrel launches and that these take 45 minutes to fill'. So that was his best guess, if you like, as to where that figure had come from.

DINGEMANS: Was he then suggesting that the 45 minutes claim was false?

WATTS: He was not suggesting it was necessarily false. But I think he was suggesting to me it might not necessarily only have one interpretation.

DINGEMANS: So that supported your view that he was a man with extraordinary access?

WATTS: Absolutely.

DINGEMANS: Did you make notes of the conversation on the 30th of May?

WATTS: I started to make notes in the same way as I usually would i.e. the shorthand aide memoire which I would note to myself the key parts and come back if I felt I wanted to. Because I was taping that conversation, I stopped after a few moments because I felt I could rely on the tape.

DINGEMANS: With what type of machine were you taping the conversation?

WATTS: This was a hand-held dictaphone, quite an old hand-held dictaphone.

DINGEMANS: Were you holding it to the receiver or did you have him on speakerphone?

WATTS: No, I had, again, quite an antiquated set-up, I suppose. It was one of these stick-on microphones attached to the receiver. Again, it was an aide-memoire to a private conversation for me to – an equivalent of notes.

DINGEMANS: And did you tell Dr Kelly that you were taping the conversation?

WATTS: No, I did not tell him.

DINGEMANS: You say: 'Okay, um, while I'm sure since you've been in New York I don't know whether you've been following the kind of the rumpus that's erupted over here … What prompted me to ring you, was the quotes yesterday on the Today Programme about the 45 minutes… 'Mr Kelly [said]: It was a statement that was made and it just got out of all proportion. They were desperate for information…that was one that popped up and it was seized on. [You say] 'Okay, just back up momentarily on the 45 minute issue. Would it be accurate then as you did in that earlier conversation to say that it was Alastair Campbell himself who…? And Dr Kelly says 'No, I can't. All I can say is the No 10 press office. I've never met Alastair Campbell so I can't. You interrupt. 'They seized on that?' Who were you referring to when you said 'they seized on that'?

WATTS: The No. 10 press office.

DINGEMANS: And [Dr Kelly] replied: 'But I think Alastair Campbell is synonymous with that press office because he's responsible for it'.

WATTS: Hmm, hmm.

DINGEMANS: Can we turn to SJW/1/53? And this is a summary of what you are going to say to the camera and indeed did say? It's really on page 54 if we can go to that, that we get any report of your conversation with Dr Kelly. It's about half way down. You introduce your anonymous source, making it clear that you cannot name him. 'Our source said…' Perhaps you can read that out?

WATTS: Yes. The direct quote from Dr Kelly is: 'That was the real concern – not so much what they had now, but what they would have in the future. But that unfortunately was not expressed strongly in the dossier, because that takes away the case for war – to a certain extent.'

DINGEMANS: Then I think at the top of page 55 [on] Newsnight, on 2nd June. Can you read those?

WATTS: 'It was a statement that was made and it just got out of all proportion. They were desperate for information, they were pushing hard for information which could be released. That was one that popped up and it was seized on, and it's unfortunate that it was. That's why there is the argument between the Intelligence Services and No. 10 – because they picked up on it and once they've picked up on it you can't pull it back from them.'

DINGEMANS: Any other comments from him?

WATTS: 'It was an interesting week before the dossier was put out because there were so many people saying, 'Well, I'm not so sure about that', or in fact that they were happy with it being in, but not expressed the way that it was – because the word-smithing is actually quite important. The intelligence community are a pretty cautious lot on the whole – but once you get people presenting it for public consumption then of course they use different words.'

DINGEMANS: And that was the material that you had obtained from your telephone conversation with Dr Kelly.

WATTS: Yes.

DINGEMANS: There came a time when the BBC paid for you to take independent legal advice through a firm of solicitors; is that right?

WATTS: I should just clarify I think why that happened.

DINGEMANS: Right.

WATTS: And it was for two reason, two important reasons. Firstly, that I felt under some considerable pressure to reveal the identity of my source.

DINGEMANS: Pressure from?

WATTS: The BBC

DINGEMANS: Yes.

WATTS: And I also felt that the purpose of that was to help corroborate the Andrew Gilligan allegations and not for any proper news purpose.

DINGEMANS: Did you consider that they corroborated Andrew Gilligan's story?

WATTS: No, I did not.

DINGEMANS: Why not?

WATTS: Because there were very significant differences between his report and my report namely, that I did not include the name of Alastair Campbell. And I did not refer to my source as being a member of the Intelligence Services and that the claim was not inserted by either Alastair Campbell himself or any member of the Government. It was for those two reasons, the pressure to identify my source and what I felt to be a misguided strategy in the use of those Newsnight reports, on which I sought independent legal advice.

DINGEMANS: Is there anything else that you would like to say to his Lordship?

WATTS: Only one thing, which is that during the process in the news suite on the Friday

DINGEMANS: The day on which Dr Kelly's body has been found?

WATTS: Everybody was very upset. There were many different concerns being juggled, sensitivities to the family, the needs of straightforward objective news reporting by the BBC. But I was concerned that it not be apparent that it was Dr Kelly's death that had prompted me to feel able to reveal his identity. It was not his death. For me when he gave evidence to the Foreign Affairs Committee, I formed a view on listening to that evidence that if I had been called to the Committee which was a possibility, I would have felt that he had relieved me of my obligation of confidence to him and I would then have felt able to reveal him as the source of my stories. And the reason for that is because under questioning he was given some – loosely quoted – the quotes from him in my reports. I saw the transcript the following day, he appears to deny that those are his quotes. I felt that together with his having acknowledged having spoken to me, although I think he was less than frank in describing the full nature of our relationship and conversations, that those factors together relieved me of my obligation to protect his identity as a confidentiality source.

Martin Howard, 14th August 2003

DINGEMANS: Mr Howard, we had a dossier on 20th June 2002. Do you recollect that?

HOWARD: Yes, I do.

DINGEMANS: We had a dossier of 5th September 2002, we had a [published] dossier on the 19th September 2002.

HOWARD: That is right, yes.

DINGEMANS: 5th September, no 45 minutes claim.

HOWARD: Hmm, hmm.

DINGEMANS: 19th September, 45 minutes.

HOWARD: Hmm, hmm.

DINGEMANS: Can I take you to DOS/2/7 [draft 10/11 September] 'Envisages the use of WMD in its current military planning, and could deploy such weapons within 45 minutes of the order being given…' Can we now look at the dossier that comes in on the 16th September? That is DOS 2/58. 'The Iraqi military may be able to deploy chemical or biological weapons within 45 minutes of an order to do so.' It seems to have got a little bit weaker; is that fair?

HOWARD: Well I was not involved in this process, it's very fine shading.

DINGEMANS: And then go to the dossier as it turned out, DOS/1/59, that his military planning allows for some of the WMD to be ready within 45 minutes of an order to use them.' This is noticeably harder, is that fair?

HOWARD: I think that is fair, yes.

DINGEMANS: These changes, which may be considered significant by intelligence personnel, you understood to be causing some of the concerns?

HOWARD: I think their concerns were about how it had been presented in the Prime Minister's foreword and in the executive summary.

DINGEMANS: Which is where, I suppose, the No.10 element became the strongest, because that was in the foreword.

HOWARD: I think that is probably true to say.

DINGEMANS: Can I then turn to other matters that I think you are going to help us with? Did you have any involvement in the broadcasts that had been made by Andrew Gilligan?

HOWARD: His broadcast on 29th May?

DINGEMANS: Yes. Did anyone contact you and ask you to undertake any investigations?

HOWARD: Yes, on 4th June the permanent secretary Kevin Tebbit wrote to the chief of defence intelligence, to identify more closely who might have been involved in passing this information to Mr Gilligan.

DINGEMANS: Did you have any other conversations at about this time?

HOWARD: Yes, it was a reception at the Security Service headquarters at Thames House, and in a conversation that I had with Mr Lamb and others it emerged that Dr Kelly had told Mr Lamb that he had spoken to Mr Gilligan –

DINGEMANS: So what did you do in response to that?

HOWARD: Well, I thought about it overnight and I decided to report this to Sir Kevin Tebbit,

DINGEMANS: You had seen Dr Kelly's letter, is that right, dated 30th June?

HOWARD: That is right.

DINGEMANS: Did you then become involved with [his] interview on 7th July?

HOWARD: Sir Kevin Tebbit was proposing to write to [the Prime Minister's security coordinator] Sir David Omand

DINGEMANS: Why had it gone up a level, as it were?

HOWARD: I think this was a judgment made by Sir Kevin Tebbit, that we had a letter which, you know, clearly showed that there had been a meeting between Dr Kelly and Andrew Gilligan, that it was clearly unauthorised, that it had certainly touched upon matters which were the subject of Andrew Gilligan's report. It was, you know, potentially quite a serious issue; Sir David recorded the Prime Minister's views that before we decided on what are the next steps that should be taken, it would be sensible to try to go into the differences between what Dr Kelly had said and what Andrew Gilligan had claimed.

DINGEMANS: Your broad understanding lower down, although not that lower down the chain, sorry, was that people at a higher level had become involved and there was then going to be a second interview?

HOWARD: Yes.

DINGEMANS: After the second interview were you convinced by what Dr Kelly had said?

HOWARD: I had no reason to doubt what Dr Kelly said. I still felt it most likely that he was the source that Andrew Gilligan had referred to.

DINGEMANS: Did you write to anyone about Dr Kelly's views as expressed in the interview?

HOWARD: I wrote to Sir John Scarlett, who is chairman of the JIC. Sir John Scarlett – not Sir John Scarlett yet. John Scarlett had asked me if I could provide a short summary of what I understood Dr Kelly's views to be on Iraqi WMD.

DINGEMANS: Right, we have got to the 8th July. You know, do you not, that the MoD issued a press statement –

HOWARD: Yes.

DINGEMANS: – saying that an undisclosed official has come forward? Do you know why it was proposed to issue a press notice?

HOWARD: I think the feeling was that this was a matter of, you know, very considerable public interest, that the Foreign Affairs Committee had themselves recommended that the Government should investigate links with Andrew Gilligan; and there was a very great concern that this would come out by other means.

HUTTON: In the report I think the F[oreign] A[ffairs] C[ommittee] said that Mr Gilligan's sources should be investigated. That would seem to suggest that the Ministry of Defence themselves would investigate that, but it does not necessarily mean, does it, that if the source was found that he would be asked to go to be a witness before the FAC?

HOWARD: No, it does not mean that automatically, my Lord, I agree. But it was part of a number of reasons, which included the fact that this was an issue or had been an issue of great public interest.

HUTTON: Yes.

HOWARD: That we had very unusually an individual who had written and said he had spoken to a journalist in this area in an unauthorised way. And the overall judgment reached, I think at all levels, from Ministers downwards, was that really it would be necessary to make the fact that this had happened public.

HUTTON: Can you just elaborate a little on that?

HOWARD: The accusation had been made that the Government had exaggerated the dossier.

HUTTON: Quite, yes. Then was the thinking that if Dr Kelly's name was made public and Dr Kelly came forward and said that he had not made the comments which Mr Gilligan had reported, that would show that Mr Gilligan's account was incorrect? Was that, in essence, the thinking?

HOWARD: It was more that this was information that was germane to an issue which had been of great public concern and great public debate.

HUTTON: But if the civil servant was not going to be named and if he was not going to give his account of what he said to Mr Gilligan, how would it advance the public knowledge to say that an unnamed civil servant had come forward?

HOWARD: Well, first of all, the fact that it had happened at all was very unusual; and there was a concern that if it came out from other sources that we might well be criticised for not having made this public. We might have been criticised for covering up for a whistle blower.

DINGEMANS: On that point. I mean, if the concern was to ensure that the public knew as much as possible, then the F[oreign] A[ffairs] C[ommittee] had actually asked for the drafts of the dossier, had they not?

HOWARD: I believe they had, yes.

DINGEMANS: Had they been given them?

HOWARD: Not to my knowledge. That is a matter for the Foreign Office to answer.

DINGEMANS: As far as the defensive Q and A material was concerned –

HOWARD: Hmm, hmm.

DINGEMANS: – this was material prepared by the Ministry of Defence to be given to their press personnel –

HOWARD: That is right.

DINGEMANS: – to brief the media with on the 8th/9th July?

HOWARD: Hmm, hmm.

DINGEMANS: Were you involved in the preparation of that at all?

HOWARD: Yes. It was discussed at the rather lengthy meeting which took place on 8th July.

DINGEMANS: What was the reasoning behind this defensive Q and A material?

HOWARD: Defensive Q and A material overall was to provide material that the press office could draw upon if they were asked questions by the media in the aftermath of the public statement.

DINGEMANS: Can I take you to MoD/1/63, which is part way through this defensive Q and A material? It says this, 'It is unprecedented for a Government Department to make a statement of this sort. Why have you done it?'

HOWARD: It was actually quite an unusual situation that we found ourselves in. So I think that really is reflected there.

DINGEMANS: Part of the reason appears to be that 'the official involved volunteered the information to us.' That is hardly likely to encourage others to do that, is it?

HOWARD: Well, I could not argue with that.

DINGEMANS: Now, on Monday 14th July we know that you took part in a briefing of Dr Kelly?

HOWARD: That is right. Sir Kevin Tebbit asked me if I would see Dr Kelly, to explain to Dr Kelly, as we would before any witnesses going before Select Committees, how Select Committees worked

DINGEMANS: Can I take you to a document which is CAB/1/106? 'DCDI' That is you, is it not?

HOWARD: That is me.

DINGEMANS: '...is to brief David Kelly this afternoon for his appearances tomorrow before the FAC and ISC, and will strongly recommend that Kelly is not drawn on his assessment of the dossier and stick to what he told Gilligan. Kelly is apparently feeling the pressure, and does not appear to be handling it well.'

HOWARD: I do not recall saying that.

DINGEMANS: Was the effect of this interview that Dr Kelly was being given a certain steer as to how his evidence should go?

HOWARD: No, certainly not.

Alastair Campbell, 19th August 2003

DINGEMANS: What is your occupation?

CAMPBELL: I am the Prime Minister's Director of Communications and Strategy.

DINGEMANS: Throughout the course of your evidence I am going to be referring to some documents that you very kindly supplied to us. You have also supplied to us copies or redacted copies of your diaries. Can you just, first of all, explain how you keep your diaries?

CAMPBELL: I write a diary not every day but several times a week. It is not intended for publication. It is a series of observations about what I do and what I witness.

DINGEMANS: When were you first aware that a dossier was being written or produced?

CAMPBELL: I had been aware for some months of a different dossier on the general issue of WMD. On the specific Iraq dossier, I became aware of that during – the intention of doing one during August, when the Prime Minister and I were both on holiday and we were discussing the way that the Iraq situation was developing.

DINGEMANS: Can you help us: what was identified as the toughest question?

CAMPBELL: Sorry: what new evidence was there? The Prime Minister said the debate had got ahead of us so we were going to do the dossier earlier, in the next few weeks. The debate, particularly in the United States, had really moved on to a different level. And what he was saying there was that any case that we make for why Saddam Hussein's regime is a serious and credible threat has to be based on evidence, and he wanted to share as much of that evidence as possible with the public.

DINGEMANS: And what did you record at the time that you needed to show in relation to the dossier?

CAMPBELL: That it had to be revelatory; we needed to show it was new and informative and part of a bigger case. I emphasised that the credibility of this document depended fundamentally upon it being the work of the Joint Intelligence Committee.

DINGEMANS: Can I then take you to a document dated 5th September? That is CAB/11/17, which was an email from Jonathan Powell to you. We start at the bottom of the page, simply working our way up in chronological sequence. You can see, 1.50, what did you decide on dossiers? And there is a first comment that has been redacted. Up the page you say: 'Regarding the dossier, substantial rewrite with JS...' Who is that?

CAMPBELL: John Scarlett [chairman of the Joint Intelligence Committee.]

DINGEMANS: John Scarlett will take to the US next Friday, and be in shape Monday thereafter. Structure as per TB's discussion.' I imagine that is the Prime Minister?

CAMPBELL: Yes.

DINGEMANS: 'Agreement that there has to be real intelligence material in their presentation as such.'

CAMPBELL: Hmm.

HUTTON: Did you receive any indication that there might have been unhappiness in the lower ranks of the intelligence agencies about the writing of the dossier, about what would be in it?

CAMPBELL: Not at that stage.

HUTTON: Yes.

DINGEMANS: If we go to DOS/2/7: 'Envisages the use of weapons of mass destruction in its current military planning, and could deploy such weapons within 45 minutes of the order being given for their use.'

CAMPBELL: Hmm, hmm.

HUTTON: You did not know where the entry of 45 minutes had come from in the sense you did not know what it was based on?

CAMPBELL: I knew it had come from the JIC but I was not aware either of the raw intelligence on which it was based or of the sourcing. What is more, I did not make any effort to find out.

HUTTON: No.

DINGEMANS: Can I just then, at the moment, come to the issue about dissatisfaction of members of the intelligence staff about some of the comments being made –

CAMPBELL: Hmm, hmm.

DINGEMANS: – and take you to an email at CAB/3/21 specific about Dr Kelly. This is 10th September [at] 11.41.

CAMPBELL: Hmm, hmm.

DINGEMANS: You can see the subject is 'Dossier – Iraq'. The person who sends it says this: 'I have just spoken to Dr David Kelly… about the growth media which Iraq claimed it used in BW work. But Iraq has not revealed its production documents therefore this amount is unaccounted for. The existing wording is not wrong – but it has a lot of spin on it'.

CAMPBELL: Hmm, hmm.

DINGEMANS: Were you aware of comments of this nature being made at the time amongst Defence Intelligence personnel?

CAMPBELL: No.

DINGEMANS: And the only other document, can I take you to MoD/4/9, which was a document which is dated in July 2003, and it is for a briefing, but this relates to concerns that were expressed contemporaneously. You can see that concerns were expressed into three main groups: recent production of [CBW] agent; the 45 minute claim; and Saddam and the importance of CBW.

CAMPBELL: Hmm, hmm.

DINGEMANS: One can see in relation to the 45 minutes claim, if I can just deal with that –

CAMPBELL: Yes.

DINGEMANS: – that concerns had apparently related to the level of certainty expressed in the foreword and executive summary.

CAMPBELL: Hmm, hmm.

DINGEMANS: That, at the least, indicates there were some people who were unhappy with some of the wording that was going on; you were not aware of that?

CAMPBELL: I was not aware of that.

DINGEMANS: Can I take you to some emails making the rounds on September 11? CAB/11/23 There is Daniel Pruce's email, it is to you and copied to others. It is subject: 'Draft Dossier (J Scarlett version of 10th September).' Daniel Pruce is?

CAMPBELL: He is a Foreign Office press officer based in Downing Street.

DINGEMANS: He said: 'The foreword is good but whose voice is it? Do we need a Minister to sign it off?' That is what starts the process running, I suppose, until the Prime Minister –

CAMPBELL: It is not actually. Danny Pruce is a very, very good press officer, but this is him making contributions effectively above his pay grade. The foreword process was already under discussion between myself, the Prime Minister, and John Scarlett.

DINGEMANS: And who had, in fact, drafted that?

CAMPBELL: I prepared a draft based upon a discussion with the Prime Minister, and with others, about what should go into that draft.

DINGEMANS: CAB/11/53. This is Jonathan Powell's email to you. I imagine his comments were comments that you took seriously, is that right?

CAMPBELL: I had certainly read them.

DINGEMANS: And he says –

CAMPBELL: Sorry, that was no offence intended there.

DINGEMANS: 'I think it is worth explicitly stating what TB keeps saying, this is the advice to him from the JIC?' He goes on to deal with this: 'We need to do more to back up the assertions.' He suggests some wording. And: 'In the penultimate paragraph you need to make it clear Saddam could not attack us at the moment. The thesis is he would be a threat to the UK in the future if we do not check him.' At page 69.

CAMPBELL: Of the dossier?

DINGEMANS: Sorry CAB/11/69. On the same day, but later on, he appears to have made some comments to John Scarlett, but he has copied you into those. Here the tone of his email seems to be slightly different to the effect that the document does nothing to demonstrate a threat. I am third line down: 'Let alone an imminent threat from Saddam in other words it shows he has the means but it does not demonstrate he has the motive to attack his neighbours let alone the west.'

CAMPBELL: Hmm, hmm.

DINGEMANS: Do you know, from any discussions you had with John Scarlett, whether those were taken up with – whether he accepted any of those, et cetera?

CAMPBELL: I think what Jonathan is doing there is making an observation which is actually consistent with what John Scarlett had been doing. I mean, this dossier is sometimes described as the Prime Minister 'making the case for war'. What it was actually doing was setting out in as factual a way as possible the reason why the Government was concerned about Saddam's WMD programmes.

DINGEMANS: Can I then take you to a document, CAB/11/70 which is a memorandum, if we go to page 71 at the bottom, you can see is from John Scarlett. Effectively the gist of what he appears to be doing is taking on some comments about strengthening the language on current concerns and plans, is that right?

CAMPBELL: I think it showed he took on some of my comments and none of the Prime Minister's on the structure. The structure stayed the same and some of the detailed points he took.

DINGEMANS: Can I turn back to CAB/11/69, with Mr Powell's comments. What he says is: 'We will need to make it clear in launching the document that we do not claim that we have evidence that he is an imminent threat.' Is there any part of the dossier that actually makes that explicitly clear?

CAMPBELL: I know that what we always said was: a serious and credible threat to the region and therefore the stability of the world.

DINGEMANS: CAB/11/103 Jonathan Powell's email at the top, the third line down says: 'Alastair, what will be the headline in the Standard on the day of publication?'

CAMPBELL: Search me.

DINGEMANS: If we look at BBC/4/90, this is what the headline was '45 Minutes From Attack'. Did you have any hand in the headline?

CAMPBELL: I did not. I do not write headlines for the Evening Standard.

DINGEMANS: Now, so you can deal with some of the points that have been suggested, did you have any influence on the inclusion of the 45 minute claim in the dossier?

CAMPBELL: None whatever. The words that you read out earlier were the words that were in the draft of the dossier that I saw on the evening of September 10th; and I had no input, output, influence upon them, whatsoever at any stage in the process.

DINGEMANS: I am proposing to move on to complaints about BBC reporting. Can I then take you to the coverage of the war in Iraq by the BBC and take you to a document at BBC/4/131. Can you tell us what this is?

CAMPBELL: (*Pause.*) This is a letter from myself to Mr Sambrook, BBC Director of News, making a number of complaints about BBC coverage during the Iraq...

DINGEMANS: 2nd April, BBC/4/149, you say: 'On Radio 4 this morning, Andrew Gilligan said …[his] final comment, was: 'I'm not quite sure where these intelligence assessments come from it might just be more rubbish from Central Command.'

CAMPBELL: Yes.

DINGEMANS: And we get the response to that at 158. Mr Sambrook had agreed that his final phrase was unacceptable and made some points about that. It does seem, looking through the file, that there were a considerable number of complaints that were being made at this time. Is that fair or unfair?

CAMPBELL: Unfair, because there was a considerable amount of coverage that was giving us cause for concern.

DINGEMANS: That is because your perception was, there was unfair or inaccurate coverage?

CAMPBELL: Yes, our perception was that BBC viewers and listeners were at times being given a sense of moral equivalence between the democratically elected governments that were involved on one side and the Iraqi regime on the other.

DINGEMANS: Can I then turn to the broadcast on 29th May? First of all, where were you on 29th May?

CAMPBELL: I was in Kuwait.

DINGEMANS: What was your reaction to those reports?

CAMPBELL: I was torn really, because, on the one hand, I did not imagine anyone would have taken them terribly seriously, because it is such an extraordinary thing to say, that the Prime Minister and the Government would do that. Given my close involvement in the production of the dossier, I knew the allegations to be false. The reason why I then got more concerned as the day wore on was because shortly after the Prime Minister spoke to

British troops when we were in Basra it was clear to me that the travelling press party were frankly more interested in this BBC story than they were in what the Prime Minister had been saying to the troops and his visit to Iraq.

DINGEMANS: On 1st June, looking at your diary, what was your reaction to all this press coverage?

CAMPBELL: I said it was grim. It was grim for me and it was grim for TB and there is this huge stuff about trust?

DINGEMANS: And did you speak to John Scarlett at all?

CAMPBELL: I did.

DINGEMANS: And what was the gist of that conversation?

CAMPBELL: The gist of that conversation was that John expressing his absolute support. Could I just add to that? I have just seen what he went on to say. He said: 'You are the brutal political hatchet man and I am the dry intelligence officer and we've been made to [ac]cord to our stereotypes'.

DINGEMANS: Mr Campbell, if you look on your screen you will see the reference is CAB/1/244. You can see there the letter you wrote to Mr Sambrook. Can you just tell us how you concluded the letter?

CAMPBELL: I predicted that he would seek to defend the story because, in my experience, Mr Sambrook generally does. I then concluded by saying that: 'On the word of a single, uncorroborated source, you have allowed one reporter to drive the BBC's coverage. We are left wondering why you have guidelines at all, given that they are so persistently breached without any comeback whatsoever.'

DINGEMANS: That seems a reasonably strong letter. Does that give proper vent to your feelings at the time?

CAMPBELL: It does.

DINGEMANS: Did you also speak with the Prime Minister about the dispute with the BBC?

CAMPBELL: Yes. Yes, I did.

DINGEMANS: And what was the gist of that discussion?

CAMPBELL: At that stage, the Prime Minister was saying to me: look, this is clearly quite an intense row that is going on. It is fine, keep going, but then we have to just after a day or two just leave this to the [Foreign Affairs] committee. During that discussion the Prime Minister was saying to me: how on earth are we going to get back on to a domestic political agenda? I said that until we could somehow change this dynamic that was currently prevalent in the media, it was going to be very difficult.

DINGEMANS: We then come on to the 8th July. The Prime Minister is prepared, in the morning, for the Commons Liaison Committee. Then at 11.30 am he returns and there is a discussion about whether or not Dr Kelly's name should be made public. Were you party to that discussion?

CAMPBELL: I was party to parts of that discussion.

HUTTON: Mr Campbell, I would just like to ask you a general question: suppose at this discussion on 8th July someone had said: let us just hold on for a minute, this is a civil servant who has given very distinguished service to his country, he has admittedly been indiscreet in speaking to a journalist as he has, but if we release his name we are going to subject him to very considerable strain. Is it right that we should do this?

CAMPBELL: I think you could have done that, but I think it would still have ended with all the media pressure because I think it would have come out, because these things do.

HUTTON: References have been made to the concern that if his name was not given to the [Foreign Affairs

Committee] and/or the [Intelligence and Security Committee] and if it leaked out, that the Government would be accused of a cover-up?

CAMPBELL: Part of the discussion that I recall involving the Prime Minister and others was about what Dr Kelly might actually say if he was called before a select committee. The Prime Minister did have some concerns about the Government's position.

HUTTON: So the concern was that if his name was not given by the Government but it was later revealed, it might transpire that Dr Kelly had views which were quite or strongly critical of the Government?

CAMPBELL: That is right.

DINGEMANS: Can I ask you on 9th July, two aspects of your diary in that respect. What was, as you perceived it, the biggest thing needed at this stage?

CAMPBELL: I felt that at that time, if we were going to bottom out this story and have it established beyond doubt that the allegations were false, then I felt that Dr Kelly appearing before a [parliamentary] Committee probably was the only way that was going to happen.

DINGEMANS: So you were keen by 9th July that Dr Kelly's name should be out?

CAMPBELL: I felt – we all felt that was going to happen, and I thought that that was the only way this was going to be resolved. But I did not do anything to bring that about because I was under strict instructions not to.

DINGEMANS: At CAB/1/93 can I take you to an email that is sent to you. You have Tom Kelly here, the Prime Minister's Official Spokesman, writing an email saying: 'This is now a game of chicken with the Beeb – the only way they will shift is [if] they see the screw tightening.' Was this the mindset that was dominating No. 10 at this stage?

CAMPBELL: I do not think it does reflect the mindset really. I think I know what Tom is saying there. I think emails that are sent between colleagues who are very close and work together very closely can look very different when you are staring at them in a screen in a courtroom.

DINGEMANS: We hear, on 17th July, that Dr Kelly goes out and his body is found the next day. Is there anything you wanted to say in relation to that

CAMPBELL: (*Pause.*) I just wanted to say that I think, like everybody, I have found it very distressing that Dr Kelly who, was clearly somebody of distinction, had died in this was and obviously I have, like everybody I am sure has thought very, very deeply about the background to all this. So I think all I would say is that I just find it very, very sad.

DINGEMANS: Is there anything further about the circumstances surrounding Dr Kelly's death that you can assist his Lordship with?

CAMPBELL: I do not think so.

HUTTON: Thank you very much Mr. Campbell. Thank you. We will sit again tomorrow morning at 10: 30.

USHER: All rise.

Houselights up to full.

James Blitz, 21st August 2003

BLITZ: My full name is James Simon Blitz.

DINGEMANS: What is your occupation?

BLITZ: The political editor of the *Financial Times* newspaper.

DINGEMANS: On 10th July you wrote an article in the *Financial Times* which named Dr Kelly as the individual who had come forward to the Ministry of Defence? Can you tell us the circumstances which led to you obtaining the name?

BLITZ: On the afternoon of Tuesday 8th July the MoD press release was published which suggested that an individual had come forward.

DINGEMANS: So what did you do when you got that press release?

BLITZ: I wrote a story for the 9th July edition of the FT.

DINGEMANS: Did that relate to Dr Kelly or not?

BLITZ: The name of Dr Kelly was not in the story that appeared on the 9th July.

DINGEMANS: Did you then carry on trying to find out who this anonymous person was?

BLITZ: I was not actively pursuing for the purposes of that article in the morning the question of who the individual was who had come forward in the MoD press release.

DINGEMANS: Did you change your attitude during the course of Wednesday 9th July?

BLITZ: Yes, I did.

DINGEMANS: Why was that?

BLITZ: Because I attended the Lobby briefing at 3.45 for Lobby journalists.

DINGEMANS: And we have an extract from that. It is at FIN/1/46. I am very sorry, it is not going to come on the screen. Can I read a short extract: 'Asked if the person who had come forward was a man, the [PM's Official Spokesman] said that journalists had a 50 per cent chance of being right. Asked whether he had been suspended from his job, he declined to get into personnel matters. Put to him that the person did not work for the MoD, the PMOS said the person was a technical expert who had worked for a variety of Government departments including the MoD with whom he was currently working, salary paid by another department.' Then some further questions. Was that the matter which had triggered your further interest?

BLITZ: That is precisely the matter that triggered my further interest and in the course of the Lobby briefing I asked a question specifically as to whether the name of the individual would in any way be publicised at some stage.

DINGEMANS: What was the answer you got?

BLITZ: The answer which was recorded in the official transcript put up on the Downing Street website was that the Prime Minister's official spokesman did not know of any plan to publicise that name.

DINGEMANS: What struck you about that briefing?

BLITZ: There were two aspects of the briefing that struck me, namely that details about this individual were coming forward; the fact that he worked for the MoD but was paid for by another department; the fact that he was a technical expert in the area of chemical and biological weapons. I took the view that there could be very few people who could fit such a description and that it would be possible to relatively quickly come to that person's name.

DINGEMANS: How did you go about trying to find the actual identity?

BLITZ: I went back to my office which is in the Parliamentary press gallery and I began to make inquiries.

DINGEMANS: What inquiries did you make?

BLITZ: Would you like me to go through this in detail at this point?

DINGEMANS: Yes, you tell me.

BLITZ: My first reaction was to open the Civil Service Handbook which lists the names of most key civil servants. The thought on my mind was that since the individual was paid for by another Government department he might be listed under such a department. I called my colleague, the FT security correspondent, in the paper's main office. I told him that I was determined to try and get the name of the individual and asked him if he would help. I called a Whitehall official and asked whether the individual worked in the DTI.

DINGEMANS: Were you given any information?

BLITZ: The only thing I wish to say about this conversation, because it was an off the record conversation, is that at the end of it I came to the conclusion that the individual was paid for by the Foreign and Commonwealth Office. I gained no other information whatsoever from that conversation.

DINGEMANS: What do you do to continue?

BLITZ: At this stage my colleague, on of the four members of the team which I lead at Westminster, came into the room.

DINGEMANS: You tell him what is going on. How does he help you?

BLITZ: Mr Adams, like myself, does not specialise in defence or intelligence work, so with very little information with which to establish the identity of the individual, he chose to conduct a search on the Internet.

DINGEMANS: Right, and he put some key words in.

BLITZ: 'Ministry', 'defence' 'consultant', 'chemical' and 'weapons'.

DINGEMANS: And who popped up on the search?

BLITZ: The first search produced a list of references where the key words appeared. Mr Adams reviewed the results of that search and told me of one individual. I looked at the name of the individual and I took the view that this was not somebody who matched the description that has been given out at the 3.45 briefing.

DINGEMANS: Right.

BLITZ: He continued his research and selected from the list the reference to www.Sussex.ac.uk which produced a document.

DINGEMANS: Was Dr Kelly's name on that document?

BLITZ: It was on that document, yes.

DINGEMANS: Had you ever heard of Dr Kelly before that?

BLITZ: No, I had not.

DINGEMANS: So what did you do to take the matter further forward?

BLITZ: Mr Adams and I concentrated our attention on that name. We proceeded to have a series of conversations with Whitehall official at the start of which we put the name of Dr David Kelly as the possible individual.

DINGEMANS: Right, and what was the first response Mr Adams got?

BLITZ: One moment please.

DINGEMANS: 44.

BLITZ: Yes I wish to be very faithful to the witness statement I have given you if I may.

DINGEMANS: Right I hope this is based on your recollection.

BLITZ: This is based on a very firm recollection and Mr Adams' recollection of what happened this afternoon. Mr Adams spoke with the first Whitehall official that he contacted. He understood the conversation to be off the record. The official declined to comment when Mr Adams put Dr David Kelly's name to that person.

DINGEMANS: Does he speak to anyone else?

BLITZ: He spoke to a second Whitehall official on the same off the record basis. The official did not confirm Dr David Kelly as the individual and referred Mr Adams to the MoD press office. Mr Adams then pursued his inquiries around the name of Dr David Kelly. Asked about Dr David Kelly's job and background, this official replied that he was seconded to the MoD from the Porton Down defence establishment and that his salary was paid by the FCO [Foreign Office].

DINGEMANS: What did Mr Adams do after that?

BLITZ: Mr Adams then tried to speak to [Miss] Pam Teare, the head of the MoD press office, on the telephone but she was engaged on another telephone call.

DINGEMANS: Following that lack of success?

BLITZ: Mr Adams spoke to a third Whitehall official on an off the record basis and pressed that person with Dr David Kelly's name. At the end of this conversation Mr Adams believed that Dr David Kelly was the individual mentioned in the MoD press statement the night before.

DINGEMANS: How was the individual actually identified?

BLITZ: It was only a few moment later that Mr Adams again called Miss Teare. He put the name of Dr David Kelly to her and she immediately confirmed he was the individual in the MoD statement.

DINGEMANS: Having confirmed the name, he obviously told you, did he?

BLITZ: That is correct.

DINGEMANS: And what did you do then?

BLITZ: I then proceeded to speak to other – to continue with inquiries. Although I had confirmation of this, you must understand this was a most unusual situation. I telephone another Whitehall official and spoke to that official on an off-the-record basis. I indicated to that person I had good grounds for believing that Dr David Kelly was the individual mentioned in the MoD statement. This official did not expressly confirm my belief, but the language used left me in no doubt that Dr David Kelly was indeed the person in question.

DINGEMANS: Did you then start to produce any article on the basis of this information?

BLITZ: I did not, at that point, do that. Before writing the article I telephone Ms Teare myself. Ms Teare told me the MoD had a policy to confirm the name to any journalist who offered it.

DINGEMANS: And then did you become aware, later on, that other journalists had identified –

BLITZ: Dr David Kelly?

DINGEMANS: Yes.

BLITZ: Around one hour after I filed the story, I was informed by a journalist on another newspaper that the *Times* and *The Guardian* had also discovered the name of the individual in the MoD press statement. This was the first moment at which I was aware of this fact.

Andrew Mackinlay MP, 26th August 2003

DINGEMANS: Could you tell his Lordship your full name.

MACKINLAY: Yes, my Lord. I am Andrew Mackinlay. I am the member of Parliament for Thurrock. I was elected in 1992 so I am in my third term.

DINGEMANS: You were party to the Foreign Affairs Committee's [decision] to investigate the decision to go to war in Iraq?

MACKINLAY: Correct an enthusiastic advocate, some were not. The reason why I was enthusiastic we should investigate this matter of the Government's justification for going to war was against a backdrop of many people, many very good people who either were opposed to war initially or then had doubts afterwards. There was currency in the press and in the political world that the Government had exaggerated the case; and it seemed to me that Parliament had a duty to look, albeit retrospectively, as to whether or not the Government had exaggerated that case. Also it is against a backdrop that for the first time in our history Parliament actually voted an affirmative resolution to commit our armed forces to a conflict situation – is has never happened before, and all 650 of us had to wrestle with our consciences. The historic duty of Parliament is one of scrutiny. It seemed to me no greater duty than to scrutinise this issue. The very final point I make on this is in a way after all the Prime Minister [has] offered no other inquiry in the open on this.

DINGEMANS: There was a meeting when it was decided to call back Dr Kelly. Did you support the idea that Dr Kelly should be called to give evidence?

MACKINLAY: I did.

DINGEMANS: Mr Hoon says [In a letter to the FAC]: 'I am prepared to agree to this on the clear understanding that Dr Kelly will be questioned only on those matters which are directly relevant to the evidence that you were given by Andrew Gilligan and not on the wider issue of Iraqi WMD and the preparation of the dossier'. Were you aware of those proposed restrictions on Dr Kelly's evidence?

MACKINLAY: Yes I was. I did not agree with them. I consider it a monumental cheek of the Secretary of State to try and tell us what we should and could inquire into.

DINGEMANS: We know that Mr Gilligan had sent some emails to members of the Committee. At BBC/13/17 we can see an email dated 30th June. This is obviously before the inquiry has completed its report.

MACKINLAY: Hmm.

DINGEMANS: 'John, as promised here is my analysis of the Campbell evidence. I've added some further notes at the bottom. Andrew.' He talks about the dodgy dossier, various questions that have been asked, et cetera. Were you aware of these communications?

MACKINLAY: No, I was not until it had come out in this Inquiry some few days ago in relation to David Chidgey MP.

DINGEMANS: What is your attitude to persons who themselves appeared before the Committee making suggestions to members of the Committee?

MACKINLAY: I think this highly inappropriate.

DINGEMANS: Can I turn to 15th July? What do you recall of Dr Kelly's appearance at the beginning of the session?

MACKINLAY: Apart from the question he was softly spoken, I thought very controlled, except for – I mention this in my witness statement – two people who accompanied him and sat immediately behind him. To me that was quite significant.

DINGEMANS: FAC/4/15 question 105, which is towards the bottom of the page. You are asking him about the journalists.

MACKINLAY: Yes.

DINGEMANS: Dr Kelly: 'I have met very few journalists'. 'Andrew Mackinlay: I heard 'few', but who are the ones in your mind's eye at this moment? What are their names? Dr Kelly: That will be provided to you by the Ministry of Defence.' This continues over the page: 'Andrew Mackinlay: No, I am asking you now. This is the high court of Parliament and I want you to tell the Committee who you met.' I think you wanted to say something in relation to that?

MACKINLAY: Yes. My Lord, if I may.

HUTTON: By all means. Do you want to look at your witness statement?

MACKINLAY: Yes. Thank you very much. It is against a backdrop – that question is against the earlier questions when I had said: Can you tell me the journalist? He said: 'see the Ministry of Defence'. I asked him again. See the Ministry of Defence. I asked him again. So I say: could you let us – by Thursday, by Thursday. He again said: the Ministry of Defence. I thought this a prevarication, unnecessary, inappropriate. It was a challenge to the whole business of Parliamentary scrutiny. You see, my Lord, just supposing in a moment, my Lord, you were to ask me a question and I said: see the chairman of my constituency party. Probably because you are a disciplined man not a muscle in your face would move. Then you asked me again and I said the same thing, my Lord, and again. Then you try and help –

HUTTON: You thought Dr Kelly should answer because he was before a Committee of Parliament?

MACKINLAY: Absolutely. Absolutely. I then went on in my witness statement: 'The power of the House to punish for contempt is well-established and its origin is probably to be found in the medieval concept of the English Parliament as a primary court of justice.'

DINGEMANS: Can I ask you some questions about your other questioning towards the end of the session? FAC/4/[25]: Perhaps you can read out your question? Number 167.

MACKINLAY: 'I reckon you are chaff; you have been thrown up to divert our probing. Have you ever felt like a fall guy? You have been set up, have you not?'

DINGEMANS: Did you consider that to be a fair question?

MACKINLAY: Yes, I do think it is; and because it is against a backdrop of where the Government had indicated they think that Dr Kelly is the sole source. He then comes along to us. He has convinced me that he is not the source – the Gilligan source, very impressively, very impressively indeed. I mean, I have had lots of hating emails and letter since. A lot of people do not understand the word 'chaff'.

DINGEMANS: What did you understand?

MACKINLAY: Well, chaff to a weapons expert is what is thrown out by our destroyers and from our fighter aircraft to deflect incoming –

DINGEMANS: Exocet missiles?

MACKINLAY: Absolutely. No offence was meant. Our Committee – the paradox, the irony was that my Committee did suffer from chaff because we were successively diverted.

HUTTON: Mr Mackinlay, may I ask you, coming back to your thought that Dr Kelly had been set up.

MACKINLAY: I do not buy this business of him coming forward voluntarily. I think by this time the heat was on.

DINGEMANS: After the hearing you pursued some Parliamentary questions, at TVP/2/15.

MACKINLAY: Yes.

DINGEMANS: We see your question: 'To ask the Secretary of State for Defence which journalists Dr Kelly has met over the past two years, for what purpose and when the meeting took place.' What was your purpose in pursuing those questions?

MACKINLAY: Because Dr Kelly, if you remember, said: ask the Ministry of Defence. That is precisely what I did do. I am tenacious, I will not be thrown off on a thing like this.

HUTTON: Yes. Thank you very much indeed.

MACKINLAY: Is that all?

DINGEMANS: Is there anything else you want to say?

MACKINLAY: There is, my Lord. I deeply regret the death of Dr Kelly. If there is any way that my questions contributed to his distress or stress, I deeply regret that, and I expressed my condolences to his wife and family. After that my Lord, I have not had dealings with any journalists. Just to complete the picture, my local newspaper had daubed on its walls, 'Kelly's blood on Mackinlay's hands'. I have shown the utmost restraint and I want to continue to do so. It is difficult. Even yesterday afternoon the Today Programme phoned up my house wanting me to go on this morning, presumably to save you the trouble of listening to me because you would have heard it on your way in my Lord. My whole basis as an MP is based upon reputation and I have not been able to hit back or to respond. But you see I am like a sprung coil this morning, my Lord. I am very, very angry because I think not only Mackinlay is at stake but the future of Parliament because, my Lord, this could go either way. Your report could either very welcomely open up a whole new vista of openness in Government or it could be used as the Hutton rules whereby it buttresses all this sort of thing in the future. I think we are at a crossroads as regard Parliament. I am desperately anxious that nobody has spoken up for Parliament. The final thing, sir –

HUTTON: I think Mr Mackinlay I should just say, as I am sure you appreciate, the Bill of Rights itself provides that the affairs of Parliament should not be commented on other than in Parliament. Therefore you will appreciate it will not be appropriate for me to express views on the affairs of Parliament. That is a matter for Parliament itself.

MACKINLAY: In a way that makes it more difficult for me to be restrained, but I will continue to be restrained. Lord Hutton, there is one final point you might want to consider. The Government refused us access to documents and to people who we all now see. The irony is that all these people and documents are given to you and I am very much pleased you have them but you also can put them on a website. If it was so critical that they should not be out in the public domain. They will not let Parliament have them; now the balloon has gone up, they are available.

Geoff Hoon MP, 27th August 2003

DINGEMANS: You are Secretary of State for Defence?

HOON: Yes, I am.

DINGEMANS: Did you have any involvement in the drafting of the dossier that was published by the Government on 24th September 2002?

HOON: I saw two drafts relatively late, and I did not offer any comments or suggest any changes to it.

DINGEMANS: Were you aware of the Defence Intelligence Staff involvement with the drafting of the dossier?

HOON: I was not aware of what specific contribution they had made.

DINGEMANS: Were you aware of any unhappiness expressed by members of the D[efence] I[intelligence] S[taff] with the dossier, either before or after publication?

HOON: Not at the time.

DINGEMANS: Can I then turn to a lunch that we have heard from Ms Watts that Dr Kelly reported having with you in about April time. Did you, in fact, have lunch with Dr Kelly at any time?

HOON: No, I did not. It is my practice from time to time to eat in the Old War Office Building canteen. On this particular occasion at the end of lunch we were approached by an official, I did not know who it was. We talked about Iraq. We discussed the Government policy, which the official said he strongly supported; and it was not a formal occasion in any sense at all. I did not know that it was Dr Kelly at the time.

DINGEMANS: We have been told about investigations that were carried out after the broadcast on 29th May. Were you aware of any of these investigations?

HOON: No, I was not.

DINGEMANS: Were you told anything about a letter that the official had written?

HOON: I was told that he had set out, in some detail, that he had had this meeting with Andrew Gilligan. The significant thing was that although he had recognised some of the things that Andrew Gilligan subsequently broadcast as being attributable to him and to his conversation, he did not believe that he was Andrew

Gilligan's single source because there were other things in the broadcast that he did not recognise.

DINGEMANS: Did you have any initial reaction to this information?

HOON: I think my first – my very first reaction was that this was something that could well lead to disciplinary proceedings. Immediately, perhaps almost at the same time, I was also concerned at the Foreign Affairs Committee hearings because any disciplinary process will take some considerable time to complete.

DINGEMANS: Did you decide, when you were talking to [your Permanent Secretary] Sir Kevin Tebbit, what to do in relation to Dr Kelly, about interviews or anything else?

HOON: Well, I did not decide because it has always been my practice, in the Ministry of Defence, to ensure that appropriate responsibilities are dealt with by appropriate people. Therefore, as far as any personnel issues were concerned, the responsibility was clearly that of the Permanent Secretary.

HUTTON: Was correcting the public record a personnel matter?

HOON: It was important to the Ministry of Defence and indeed to the Government as a whole that the public record should be corrected.

DINGEMANS: Did you speak to Mr Campbell about your initial reactions on hearing the news of Dr Kelly coming forward?

HOON: Yes, I did. I emphasised to him my concern about any suggestion that the Government should be covering up [to the Foreign Affairs Committee] the fact of a potential witness coming forward.

DINGEMANS: We know that there was a draft press statement, prepared by the Ministry of Defence, and draft

Q and A material, also prepared. Were you any part of this Q and A material and were you consulted about it?

HOON: No, I was not.

HUTTON: Before we proceed, may I just ask, Secretary of State: with regard to the BBC, suppose you had given in confidence to the BBC Dr Kelly's name and that the BBC had then confirmed that: yes, he was Mr Gilligan's source. What was your thinking after that? What did you think might happen or that you might bring about?

HOON: He could indicate what he had and had not said to Andrew Gilligan, so the public, Parliament, we would all have been in a position to know whether Andrew Gilligan had or had not exaggerated the material that he had been provided with by Dr Kelly.

HUTTON: Yes. But that would have involved Dr Kelly coming forward into the public domain and stating what he had said and what he had not said to Mr Gilligan?

HOON: I was not aware that Dr Kelly necessarily had any concerns about his identity remaining secret.

DINGEMANS: Were you aware of any doubts being expressed about whether Dr Kelly had told the whole story, at this stage?

HOON: I was not aware doubts were being expressed.

DINGEMANS: Right. We can see that the Ministry of Defence are preparing some press statements. But these are now being at least altered or improved by Downing Street. Were you aware that Downing Street was involved in helping the Ministry of Defence with their press statements?

HOON: I was not directly aware of that, but it would not be a particular surprise given the involvement of Downing Street in these events.

DINGEMANS: At this stage, did you understand whether or not Dr Kelly was happy for his name to be given to any newspaper or press statement?

HOON: That, at that stage, obviously had not been discussed with Dr Kelly.

DINGEMANS: We have seen the defensive Q and A material that was actually deployed. Can I take you to some draft Q and A material which we have received, CAB/21/5 – If you can look down to the fifth question: 'Is it X (i.e. the correct name)? 'If the correct name is put to us we will need to tell the individual we are going to confirm his name before doing so? The actual Q and A material put out later has a rather different look to it. If you look at MoD/1/62, you can see: 'If the correct name is given, we can confirm it…' That is a reasonably substantial change. One is saying: we need to go back to the individual and tell him first. Do you know whether or not Dr Kelly was told about the draft Q and A material and the Q and A material as deployed?

HOON: I do not, no. But can I make clear that I did not see either of these documents.

DINGEMANS: We have heard about some meetings that took place in Downing Street on 8th July, when it is decided that Dr Kelly's name ought to be supplied to the Intelligence and Security Committee, copied to the FAC, and because it is going to be copied to the FAC, it is going to be made public. Were you being told at all what was being decided at the meeting in Downing Street?

HOON: I was certainly told that there was a proposal to contact the I[ntelligence] S[ecurity] C[ommittee] and to use the ISC as a means of perhaps persuading the BBC to reveal privately their source.

HUTTON: May I ask you, Secretary of State, did you understand that there was any thought that the ISC would go rather beyond that and would examine Dr Kelly for the purpose of coming to the conclusion that Mr Gilligan's main criticism was incorrect?

HOON: I was not present at that meeting, but what I understood to be the case was that by giving the name of Dr Kelly to the ISC on our side might encourage the BBC to reveal their source on their side. The fall back was for me to write to the BBC and to publicise the fact that an official had come forward.

DINGEMANS: Whose plan or strategy was it, as far as you understood?

HOON: I was given a message to the effect that it was now appropriate for me to write to the Chairman of the governors.

DINGEMANS: The fall back plan is coming to you from No. 10?

HOON: Yes.

HUTTON: Is it your evidence, Secretary of State, that this MoD statement was issued solely for the purpose of trying to persuade the BBC to reveal its source or was there another reason behind it?

HOON: That was certainly part of it, but throughout I had been concerned that we were in possession of significant information about a potential witness relevant to Parliamentary proceedings, relevant to the public debate.

DINGEMANS: Effectively there are a number of pieces of information which are going to assist any journalist to identify Dr Kelly. Is that a fair analysis of this defensive Q and A material?

HOON: I did not see this Q and A and played no part in its preparation.

DINGEMANS: Going to your correspondence with [chairman of the BBC governors] Mr Davies. You give the name, in confidence, to Mr Davies of Dr Kelly. What is the purpose behind this correspondence?

HOON: By then I had accepted that the BBC were not going to volunteer the name of their source. I thought it might assist them in assessing the reliability of what Andrew Gilligan might have said to them to indicate privately to Gavyn Davies the name of the official who had come forward.

DINGEMANS: Did you get any assistance from anyone else about [the] decision to put Dr Kelly before both the ISC and the FAC? Were you aware of anyone else's views?

HOON: I was certainly aware that the Prime Minister took the view that it would be extraordinarily difficult to explain to Parliament and to the Foreign Affairs Committee why we were refusing permission for an official who clearly had something relevant to say about their previous deliberations, why we would refuse permission for him to appear before that select committee.

DINGEMANS: How had you been aware of the Prime Minister's views in relation to that?

HOON: I had not spoken to him directly. I think that came in a view from Jonathan Powell.

DINGEMANS: Were you aware that Dr Kelly had some views that might be considered uncomfortable on the dossier and Iraqi weapons of mass destruction?

HOON: This was just one official who had particular views. But his views were not characteristic of the policy that the Government had developed or established.

DINGEMANS: We know that Dr Kelly's body was found on 18th July. Can I take you to TVP/3/238, which is an interview with Peter Sissons. Mr Sissons says this: 'This is a very great personal tragedy. He killed himself after your department, indeed you personally outed him as the probable mole.' You say this: 'We followed very carefully established MoD procedures, and at all stages, certainly as far as I personally was concerned, we protected his anonymity.' We have heard that in fact the department confirmed his name to journalists. We have heard from you that the department issued a press statement to the effect that a man had come forward, all at a time when no-one knew for sure that he was the single source. Do you still hold by your answer that the Ministry of Defence followed established procedures and protected his anonymity?

HOON: Yes, I do.

Wing Commander John Clark, 27th August 2003

KNOX: Could you tell the Inquiry your full name and your occupation?

CLARK: My name is Wing Commander John Clark. I am a Wing Commander in the Royal Air Force. My current job title is CPAC, CONAC 1.

KNOX: CPAC, am a right in thinking, stands for Counter Proliferation Arms Control?

CLARK: Correct, and the CONAC stands for Conventional Arms Control.

KNOX: I want to ask you one or two questions about your contact with Dr Kelly.

CLARK: Yes. We worked quite closely because he really was the fount of all knowledge in respect of Iraq.

KNOX: Can I ask you about Dr Kelly's press contacts. Were you aware he had a number of press contacts?

CLARK: Yes. In fact he made no secret of that fact. He was quite proud that he had many press contacts, from diverse backgrounds.

KNOX: Did you at any point before the hearing in front of the FAC discuss the forthcoming appearance with him?

CLARK: I felt it would be inappropriate to ask him the obvious questions that clearly the hearings were there to ask him. I asked him how he felt. He was tired. He was clearly not looking forward to the hearings.

KNOX: What was the atmosphere, as far as you could tell, at the Foreign Affairs Committee hearing?

CLARK: It was uncomfortable to – certainly from where I was sat it was extremely warm. The fans or the air conditioning had to be switched off because the Committee could not hear David – Dr Kelly, and they were continually asking could he speak up, speak up. He was quite a softly spoken individual, and he was obviously having difficulty being heard.

KNOX: Did Dr Kelly comment on any of the questions that he had been asked?

CLARK: Yes. He was totally thrown by the question or the quotation that was given to him from Susan Watts. He spoke about that when he came back to the office. He did say that threw him. He had not expected or anticipated that that would have come to the fore at that forum.

KNOX: Can you be a bit more precise about what that question was?

CLARK: A member of the Committee read out a very long quotation from Susan Watts which apparently David or Dr Kelly had said. Now, in response to that Dr Kelly said it was not his quote.

KNOX: So after the hearing he says to you: that really threw me?

CLARK: Yes he did.

KNOX: There has been some speculation that perhaps Mr Mackinlay was a bit brusque with him. Did he mention anything about that?

CLARK: No, I think Dr Kelly accepted he was doing his job.

KNOX: And Thursday 17th July, did Dr Kelly come into work?

CLARK: No, he did not. We had two Parliamentary Questions that had to be responded to that had been tabled by Andrew Mackinlay.

KNOX: These were the two Parliamentary Questions that you or Dr Kelly were trying to answer on the 17th?

CLARK: Yes they are.

KNOX: Did you play any part in assisting Dr Kelly to answer these Parliamentary Questions?

CLARK: Yes, I played the role of facilitator. What had been agreed on the previous day, the 16th, was Dr Kelly would provide the detail that was required by about 10 o'clock the next morning.

KNOX: Could you go to MoD/20/12? This appears to be an email from Dr Kelly to you sent at 9.22.

CLARK: Correct.

KNOX: You will see it says: John: 'I have compiled the information as best I can. The list of journalists is the most difficult because some may date before 2002 and some may have nothing to do with Iraq whatsoever.' Could you go to MoD/20/12? This appears to be an email from Dr Kelly to you sent at 9.22.

CLARK: Correct.

KNOX: You will see it says: 'John: I have compiled the information as best I can. The list of journalists is the most difficult because some may date before 2002 and some may have nothing to do with Iraq whatsoever.' Over the page he lists the journalists he has contact with.

CLARK: Yes. So I added the detail in accordance with Dr Kelly's email.

KNOX: There is another set of emails at MoD/20/22. You see here another email which you are sending at 13.59. You are now sending it to Parliamentary Questions. Who is that?

CLARK: That is the organisation we send completed Parliamentary Questions to.

KNOX: We know there appears to be another draft which you can see at MoD/20/27. There is a reference to 'journalists whose business cards Dr Kelly has in his possession.' Did you talk to Mr Kelly about this at all?

CLARK: Yes. It was decided that the reference to the business cards would remain.

KNOX: Can you recall what conversations you had with Dr Kelly in the course of the 17th July, apart from the emails?

CLARK: We had a number of calls. The first one was about 10 o'clock in the morning to say the information required is on the Internet machine. We also had a general discussion of developments, how he was feeling. He was feeling still tired but in good spirits, although at that stage – and David Kelly was a very private man and very rarely mentioned his family – he had come in later on the 16th [July] because of a personal problem at home. That was because he had obviously come back from Cornwall and his wife had been left in Cornwall and he some way had to work out how to get his wife, who has arthritis, back from Cornwall. That is why he had been making arrangements on the 16th and that is why he was somewhat later in. On the 17th, when I asked him how he was going, he basically said he was holding up all right but it had all come to a head and his wife had taken it really very badly. Whether that was in association with the additional pressure of having to get back the day before under her own steam, I do not know, but he did say that his wife had been very upset on the morning of the 17th.

KNOX: In the course of these conversations were you told by anyone that any further contacts with journalists had to be checked with Dr Kelly?

CLARK: Yes, I was contacted by the Secretary of State's office and he brought up the subject of the article that had been published on 13th July, written by Nick Rufford [of the *Sunday Times*]. Now, Dr Kelly had made no reference to that meeting in his one-to-one meetings, and I was asked to check with Dr Kelly if that meeting had taken place and, if it had, then really it ought to be included in the response.

KNOX: At what time did you attempt to ring Dr Kelly?

CLARK: It was – I have since been told by the police – I thought it was close to 3 o'clock but it was about 3.20, and I was told by his wife who answered the telephone that Dr Kelly had gone for a walk at 3 o'clock.

KNOX: Can you recall what the last telephone conversation you actually had with Dr Kelly was before that attempt to get hold of him?

CLARK: Yes, I had a call with him which was just before 3 o'clock. That was the one where we discussed the business cards.

KNOX: And after you had not been able to get hold of Dr Kelly, what did you do?

CLARK: I was surprised that I could not get two-way with him because he was always very proud of his ability to be contacted. He took his mobile phone everywhere.

KNOX: Did you try again?

CLARK: I rang his wife because clearly I needed to get the staff work taken forward and I needed to speak to Dr Kelly. I spoke to her and said I had not been able to contact Dr Kelly on his mobile and I thought she might say something but she was quite matter of fact and said, you know – did not really record the fact. I then said: could you ask Dr Kelly when he returns, could he give me a ring. That is how the message was left with his wife.

Gavyn Davies, 28th August 2003

DAVIES: My name is Gavyn Davies, I am the Chairman of the BBC.

DINGEMANS: Did you hear the broadcast by Mr Gilligan on 29th May?

DAVIES: I did. I heard the whole of the Today Programme.

DINGEMANS: Do you listen to it every morning then?

DAVIES: I do, I am afraid, yes. Not always from 6 o'clock, but –

DINGEMANS: At the time, as a member of the listening public but perhaps paying more attention than others might, what was your understanding of the original thrust of the story?

DAVIES: Well, my understanding of the thrust of the story was that Mr Gilligan was saying that he had a source who he believed to be a senior and reliable and credible source, who believed that the September 2002 dossier on intelligence had been sexed up by No. 10. There was no mention of Alastair Campbell, I seem to remember. And that some of the information in the dossier was not fully approved by the Intelligence Services.

DINGEMANS: We have heard from the Prime Minister about the denials that were issued and his hope that the story would go away with those denials.

DAVIES: Yes.

DINGEMANS: Were you aware of those denials being reported, et cetera?

DAVIES: Yes. I was aware that the Prime Minister and others, I think Alastair Campbell too, had that week said things to the effect that the programme – that the report was rubbish.

DINGEMANS: Right. But as a Chairman of Governors, are you involved at that stage?

DAVIES: No, I mean essentially I have to say that at that stage I thought that the Gilligan reports were just another of those episodes which Today tends to trip over occasionally.

HUTTON: What do you mean Mr Davies by appear to trip over?

DAVIES: What I mean is the programme – it is probably Britain's leading forum for political debate. It is a programme which attracts enormous attention; and from time to time it becomes the centre of that debate. That is really all I meant.

HUTTON: It is just the words 'trip over', if you could just explain what you mean by trip over?

DAVIES: I think I meant encountered, my Lord.

DINGEMANS: Then Mr Gilligan, continuing with the chronology if I may, giving evidence to the Foreign Affairs Committee on 19th June. Mr Campbell gives evidence on 25th June. What was your view about Mr Campbell's evidence on the debate between the Government and the BBC?

DAVIES: I mean, I felt this was an extraordinary moment. I felt it was an almost unprecedented attack on the BBC to be mounted by the head of communications at 10 Downing Street. Mr Campbell accused the BBC of lying directly. He alleged that the BBC had accused the Prime Minister of lying, something which I never believed the BBC had done. And he accused the BBC of having followed an anti-war agenda before, during and after the Iraqi conflict.

DINGEMANS: We know that Mr Campbell wrote Mr Sambrook a letter of 26th June. He asked for a response to some specific questions, I will go straight to the response which was on the 27th of June, CAB/1/355. Were you a party to this letter of response?

DAVIES: No I was not a party to that, I was aware Richard Sambrook showed me the letter from Alastair Campbell. He also showed me a draft of the reply he was going to send.

DINGEMANS: Can I take you to page 7 of the letter. And [one of] the questions that Mr Campbell had asked: 'Does the BBC still stand by the allegation it made on 29th May that No. 10 added in the 45 minute claim to the dossier?' [Answer] : 'The allegation was not made by the BBC but by our source – a senior official involved in the compilation of the dossier – and the BBC stands by the reporting of it.' There is a distinction between the BBC and the source. Was that how you saw it at the time?

DAVIES: I read this letter, Mr Dingemans, I did not write it. I believe that what this letter was doing was giving, on behalf of BBC management, our best and most truthful explanation to Mr Campbell of what we had reported.

DINGEMANS: This is when you have also decided to call a Governors' meeting. Did it become apparent that the matter was not going to go away?

DAVIES: Well, I was hoping it might go away, but in this period the Government continued in its press briefings daily, at No. 10, to bring the matter up with a fairly high degree of volume.

HUTTON: Did the Governors know that the first part of Mr Gilligan's report on 29th May was unscripted?

DAVIES: I believe they did, my Lord, yes.

HUTTON: Does that make any difference to the question of editorial control?

DAVIES: Well, I think it raises an issue. It does raise an issue, in my mind, about whether reports of this nature should be unscripted.

HUTTON: Yes.

DINGEMANS: Then you put on record [in a press release] that the BBC had not accused the Prime Minister of lying.

DAVIES: Yes. Here is a very, very strong statement and extremely unusual statement for the Board of Governors to make.

HUTTON: If you were satisfied that the Prime Minister was not lying, might it not have called for perhaps even a qualified withdrawal of the first part of the report?

DAVIES: Well, my Lord, I did not think that the BBC had any evidence to suggest that the source would have wished to withdraw his views. Now, sometimes in life you get the same event being watched by two different people with two different interpretations of the same event.

HUTTON: Quite. Yes.

DINGEMANS: You get a letter on 8th July. Can I take you to MoD/1/66 from Mr Hoon. 'Dear Gavyn, 'I am writing to draw your attention to an MoD statement which we shall be issuing later today... 'You will see that we have not named the official... We would, however, be prepared to disclose his name to you in confidence... in the interests of resolving what has become a management problem for both our organisations.' What was your reaction to that?

DAVIES: At the time I was puzzled by what he meant by management problem. I did not really know what the tactics or strategy lying behind the letter was. In any event, I could not have disclosed the name myself because I did not know the name.

DINGEMANS: Was there any correspondence after that?

DAVIES: Yes. First of all, on this one, Mr Dingemans, my suspicions that something was up were raised when I found out that the letter from Mr Hoon to myself had been released to the press, and that made me more suspicious about that, maybe something was going on that I had not fathomed.

DINGEMANS: Was there any reason that you felt that the source should not be confirmed?

DAVIES: Well, at this particular stage he had not named the source to me. He did that the following day

DINGEMANS: Can I take you to his letter of the following day? MoD/1/71.

DAVIES: Yes.

DINGEMANS: He now gives you the name Dr Kelly. So what is wrong, now, with saying: yes, it is Dr Kelly?

DAVIES: Well, I think what was wrong was first of all I did not, of course, know yet whether Dr Kelly was the source. So I was unable to confirm or deny it. What occurred to me here was: look, I do not know whether Dr Kelly is actually Mr Gilligan's source, but if he is he has probably said some very different things to Mr

Gilligan to what he has said to his employer; and my feeling was that if we had come forward and said: yes actually that is the source, we would have been betraying the confidence, number 1, because the source had never suggested that we should divulge his name, and number 2 we would have effectively been telling his employer that he had told Mr Gilligan more than he was now owning up to [to] his employer.

DINGEMANS: So what steps did you take to deal with the letter?

DAVIES: What I did was I was the only person that saw the name 'David Kelly'. I Tipexed that out and I showed the redacted letter to the Director General; and I think within a very short time we heard that the name of David Kelly was circulating among journalists and, you know, I did not know how that had happened.

DINGEMANS: Dr Kelly comes to give evidence to the Foreign Affairs Committee on 15th July. We have heard about that. We have also seen, now, an email that Mr Gilligan has sent that is FAC/6/62 and he was suggesting some questions for Dr Kelly. If you go down to the bottom of the page you can see: 'He told my colleague Susan Watts, science editor of Newsnight…' If you read that as a lay person you might think that he is suggesting that Dr Kelly was Susan Watts' source. Did you know of this email?

DAVIES: I had absolutely no idea whatsoever, no.

DINGEMANS: And what is your view on journalists sending this type of email to members of the Foreign Affairs Committee?

DAVIES: I think this is something the Director General may wish to look at.

DINGEMANS: Is there anything else that you know of the circumstances surrounding Dr Kelly's death that you can assist his Lordship with?

DAVIES: I think on behalf of the whole BBC I would like to put on record that we enormously regret the death of Dr Kelly. The BBC has the deepest sympathy for Dr Kelly's family; and all of us in the BBC are profoundly sorry about the tragic events of the last two months and we will do our utmost to learn important lessons for the future.

HUTTON: Thank you very much indeed, Mr Davies.

Dr Brian Jones, 3rd September 2003

HUTTON: Sit down please.

DINGEMANS: Can you tell his Lordship your full name.

JONES: It is Brian Francis Gill Jones.

DINGEMANS: What is your occupation?

JONES: I am a retired civil servant.

DINGEMANS: Before you retired?

JONES: I was a branch head in the Scientific and Technical Directorate of the Defence Intelligence Analysis Staff.

DINGEMANS: What is your personal opinion about weapons of mass destruction?

JONES: My personal opinion is that almost all – almost all – nuclear weapons truly fit this concept of being a weapon of mass destruction, that some biological weapons are perhaps reasonably described in that way because they could be used to produce very large numbers of casualties on the same sort of scale perhaps even as nuclear weapons, but there are many biological weapons that struggle to fit into that. Some are incapacitants for example rather than lethal.

DINGEMANS: Those are biological weapons you think do not fit into that character. What about the chemical weapons?

JONES: I think chemical weapons almost struggle to fit into that category. There are certain agents and certain scenarios where I would think that chemical weapons truly are describable as weapons of mass destruction. Sorry, could I take a sip of water?

DINGEMANS: Yes of course.

HUTTON: Do I gather, Dr Jones, that there is perhaps some debate in intelligence circles then about the precise meaning of 'weapons of mass destruction'? You are expressing your own view. Do I take it that there are others that might take a different view?

JONES: There may be. I mean, I think 'weapons of mass destruction' has become a convenient catch-all which, in my opinion, can at times confuse discussion of the subject.

HUTTON: Yes I see. Thank you, yes.

DINGEMANS: Mr Scarlett, I think, told us that Dr Kelly may have been confused about the difference between missile delivery of chemical weapons and artillery delivery. Do you think there is a difference between the two.

JONES: In terms of weapons of mass destruction? I think I would struggle to describe either as a true weapon of mass destruction.

DINGEMANS: Do you know whether Dr Kelly had seen the earlier drafts of the dossier?

JONES: I discovered on 18th September, when I met him then, that he was actually looking at the latest draft at that time.

DINGEMANS: Did you discuss with Dr Kelly his view of the dossier as so far drafted?

JONES: At that point, I did. He said he thought it was good.

DINGEMANS: And were there others in your group who had differing views?

JONES: Some of my staff had said that they were unhappy with all the detail that was in the dossier. My expert analyst on C[hemical] W[arfare] expressed particular concern. I had, I think, at the time I spoke to David, begun to look at his problems, to look at the bits of the dossier that he had problems with.

DINGEMANS: And what was your CW expert's particular concern?

JONES: Well, at its simplest he was concerned that some of the statements that were in the dossier did not accurately represent his assessment of the intelligence available to him.

HUTTON: May I just pursue: changes had been suggested. Is it your understanding they were passed on to the assessment staff but they were not adopted?

JONES: That is correct.

DINGEMANS: And those concerns had not been accepted?

JONES: Some had, but there were significant ones that had not been accepted.

DINGEMANS: And how did your CW expert feel about that?

JONES: He was very concerned.

HUTTON: Could you just elaborate a little on his concern?

JONES: My Lord, they were about language but language is the means by which we communicate an assessment, so they were also about the assessment, yes.

HUTTON: Quite. Yes.

JONES: I mean, if I can just refer to a note I have here…they were really about a tendency in certain areas, from his point of view, to shall we say over-egg certain assessments in relation particularly to the production of CW agents and weapons since 1998. And he was concerned that he could not point to any solid evidence of such production.

DINGEMANS: Did any of the personnel who were working under you know that people within the communications side of No. 10 had been making suggestions on the dossier?

JONES: I think there was an impression that they were involved in some way.

DINGEMANS: The 45 minutes is the next area. Were you aware of any concerns about the 45 minutes?

JONES: Yes, I had some concerns about the 45 minute point myself; yes. My concerns were that Iraq's chemical weapons and biological weapons capabilities were not being accurately represented. In particular, I had seen – on the advice of my staff, I was told that there was no evidence that significant production had taken place either of chemical warfare agent or chemical weapons. We had problems about the source. Our concern was that what we were hearing was second-hand information. And the information did not differentiate between whether these were chemical weapons or whether they were biological weapons; and that is an important matter. There was a lack of detail on whether the agents, the weapons, what scenarios were being discussed. It was a fairly nebulous general statement that concerned us.

DINGEMANS: Can I take you to one final reference, CAB/29/15? This was Mr A's email. Just at the bottom Mr A makes the comment: 'Another example supporting our view that you and I should have been more involved in this than the spin merchants of this administration.' Was there a perception, right or wrong, amongst D[efence] I[ntelligence] S[ervice] personnel that spin merchants were involved with the dossier?

JONES: Well, 'spin merchants' is rather emotive. I think there was an impression that there was an influence from outside the intelligence community.

DINGEMANS: And were people in the intelligence community happy with that?

JONES: No.

Janice Kelly, 1st September 2003

HUTTON: Good morning Mrs Kelly. As I think you know, Mr Dingemans will take you through your evidence and if at any time you would like a break, please just say so.

KELLY: Thank you, my Lord.

DINGEMANS: Mrs Kelly, I hope you can see me. We can see a still picture of you. Can you hear me clearly?

KELLY: I can see you and hear you.

DINGEMANS: You married Dr Kelly in 1967?

KELLY: That is correct.

DINGEMANS: Where had you met?

KELLY: We had met when he was at Leeds University. I was studying at Birmingham Training College at the time before I moved on to Birmingham University.

DINGEMANS: Mrs Kelly, you will need to keep your voice up a wee bit, if that is all right.

KELLY: That is fine.

DINGEMANS: After university, what had he gone on to do?

KELLY: He went on to do a Doctorate at Oxford University.

DINGEMANS: Do you know what that was in?

KELLY: Not entirely. It was something to do with viruses and insect viruses.

DINGEMANS: Dr Kelly was asked to get involved in the UNSCOM, United Nations Special Commission on Iraq. And we have heard that in 1988 the UNSCOM inspectors were removed from Iraq.

KELLY: That is right.

DINGEMANS: And what was his view on that?

KELLY: Yes, he felt that his job there was not finished, that Iraq did indeed have plenty of weapons to discuss and to reveal. It was quite a frustrating time I think when they were effectively thrown out of Iraq.

DINGEMANS: And it seems at about that time that he had started working more directly for the Ministry of Defence. Were you aware of that?

KELLY: It was always a bit unclear as to who he was working for. Sometimes he would be paid for some things by the Foreign and Commonwealth Office and sometimes by the United Nations.

DINGEMANS: We have heard at some time Dr Kelly became a member of the Baha'i faith. Do you know anything about that?

KELLY: Only a little. He kept it very privately to himself. It was a few years ago, perhaps five or six years ago, when I realised he was reading the Koran and he was becoming perhaps gentler in his ways, in some ways. It really was a spiritual revelation for him.

DINGEMANS: How was his mood in January time?

KELLY: In January time he was a little more tired than he had been. It was fine. He had some trepidation though about the war coming up. He believed in it but was obviously sad that we seemed to be moving towards that position.

DINGEMANS: And had he talked about his retirement, at that stage?

KELLY: Yes, but only in general terms. He was a little bit worried about his pension requirements there and we still had a mortgage to pay on the house, so he was going to leave it as late as he could.

DINGEMANS: And do you know what he was doing work-wise then?

KELLY: He was working at the United Nations.

DINGEMANS: And did he take any other holiday time, so far as you are aware?

KELLY: No, he was not good at holidays. He was always on call. He always had his mobile phone on and he took a minimum amount of time. He would try to slot in his gardening duties, mowing the lawns and so on between work, either in the evening or very occasionally he would take a day in lieu.

DINGEMANS: Did he have a weekend earlier on this year?

KELLY: Yes, he did. Our field and the lawns had got very, very long and he seemed to be driven. He really had to spend a long time doing that and he was extremely tired afterwards. We have a very old, battered ride-on mower and that was a seven hour job, and he made himself stick at it all day with just breaks for water and food. He was extremely tired. This was fitted in tightly between two visits.

DINGEMANS: In May we have heard that he met Mr Gilligan, on 22nd May. Were you aware of that meeting?

KELLY: Yes.

DINGEMANS: He did not tell you the nature of the meeting?

KELLY: No, he would never tell me the nature of his meetings.

DINGEMANS: On 30th June we know that Dr Kelly wrote a letter to his line manager. Were you aware of that at the time?

KELLY: Not at the time, no. The only thing I was aware of was that he became very much more taciturn. He became withdrawn and we as a family expressed this worry to each other, we each noticed it.

DINGEMANS: When can you date that from, if you can?

KELLY: The last week of June, I would think. We were worried about him before then. He was tired and looking his age. He seemed to have aged quite a bit.

DINGEMANS: We also know between 5th and 11th June he went out to Baghdad.

KELLY: That is right. He was really glad to be going. He was slightly nervous of what he might find there. He knew it was an occupied country. So a little bit of trepidation.

DINGEMANS: Had he enjoyed his trip?

KELLY: Yes and no. He came back with mixed feelings. So much had changed, he was quite sad for the Iraqis.

DINGEMANS: Was there anything that you noticed at the end of June, any long walks or anything?

KELLY: Yes, yes. He worried me somewhat one evening, by suddenly getting up from his chair, having been quite withdrawn and worried I think. He said he was going to walk to the Hind's Head at the other end of the village and off he went, seeming very preoccupied. That again would have been just before that letter was sent. About half an hour later he came back and I said: 'You have been quick' and he replied: 'I went for a walk instead to think something through.' He said it slowly. I immediately thought perhaps he was worrying about me or something. So he said: 'No, no, it is not you, it is a professional thing' I said: 'Do you want to talk about it?' He said no.

DINGEMANS: That brings us, I think, to 4th July. We know from documents we have seen that Dr Kelly was interviewed on 4th July about the letter he had written on 30th June.

KELLY: Right.

DINGEMANS: Did you know about that at the time?

KELLY: No, I was totally unaware of anything other than the feeling that he was not enjoying his work so much, that he was more withdrawn.

DINGEMANS: He was travelling back home on the Tuesday 8th July. How did he seem then?

KELLY: Quiet. I was busy. I was busy interviewing some people for my local History Society. So I did not actually talk to him for long at that immediate point on his return. It was a little bit later we spoke.

DINGEMANS: What was said?

KELLY: Well, we had a meal. He seemed a little bit reluctant to come and watch the news. The main story was a source had identified itself. Immediately David said to me 'it's me'.

DINGEMANS: The story, we have seen a press statement that was put out by the Ministry of Defence on 8th July, was that the story that was on the television?

KELLY: That is right. My reaction was total dismay. My heart sank. I was terribly worried because the fact that he had said that to me, I knew then he was aware his name would be in the public domain quite soon.

DINGEMANS: How did he seem to you?

KELLY: Desperately unhappy about it, really really unhappy about it. Totally dismayed. He mentioned he had had a reprimand at that stage from the MoD but they had not been unsupportive, were his words. I deliberately at that point said: would it mean a pension problem, would it mean you having to leave your job? He said it could be if it got worse, yes.

DINGEMANS: And what was his reaction to the fact that he thought his name was going to become public?

KELLY: Total dismay.

HUTTON: Did he say, Mrs Kelly, why he thought his name might or would become public?

KELLY: Yes. Because the MoD had revealed that a source had made itself known, he, in his own mind, said that he knew from that point that the press would soon put two and two together.

DINGEMANS: On the 9th July, do you know where he was?

KELLY: Yes. He was supposed to be going to London so I was quite surprised when he said he was going to work in the garden all day.

DINGEMANS: Did you have any visitors that day?

KELLY: Yes, we did in the evening. It turned out to be Nick Rufford [of the *Sunday Times*]. No journalist just turned up before this, so I was extremely alarmed by this.

DINGEMANS: And did you speak with Dr Kelly after the conversation?

KELLY: Yes, I did. He came over to me and said that Nick had said that Murdoch had offered hotel accommodation for both of us away from the media spotlight in return for an article by David. He, David, was to be named that night and that the press were on their way in droves.

DINGEMANS: And did you get the impression that he was happy or unhappy that this press statement had been made?

KELLY: Well, he did not know about it until after it had happened. So he was – I think initially he had been led to believe that it would not go into the public domain. He had received assurances and that is why he was so very upset about it.

DINGEMANS: Having heard that the press were on their way in droves, what did you do?

KELLY: We hovered a bit. I said I knew a house that was available to us if we needed it in the south west of England. The phone rang and he went in to answer it, came out, and he said: I think we will be needing that house after all. The MoD press office have just rung to say we ought to leave the house and quickly so that we would not be followed by the press. We immediately went into the house and packed and within about 10 minutes we had left the house.

DINGEMANS: You set off down to Cornwall I think? Which town did you drive to?

KELLY: Weston-Super-Mare. We had a rather sleepless night but we stayed overnight there en route to Cornwall.

DINGEMANS: You were staying in a hotel?

KELLY: We were. We had asked for *The Times* to be delivered. We just read it as we finished our breakfast. We just read a couple of articles that were about David.

DINGEMANS: What were the articles about David saying?

KELLY: There was a run down of his career given I presume by an MoD source naming him as a middle-ranking official.

DINGEMANS: How did Dr Kelly seem about that?

KELLY: Well, there was several references to his lowly status. I do not know whether it was more my reaction or his but he was rather knocked back by that. I was trying to say to him how nice Cornwall was. I was trying to make conversation to relax him and try and turn this in some way into a holiday. On the Friday we decided to go to the Lost Gardens of Heligan. We spent a long morning there during which he had taken a call from several people from MoD explaining about the Foreign Affairs Committee on the Tuesday. One was from Bryan Wells. Who told him it would be televised.

DINGEMANS: How did Dr Kelly take that news?

KELLY: He was ballistic. He just did not like that idea at all. He felt it – he did not say this in so many words but he felt it would be a kind of continuation of a kind of reprimand into the public domain.

DINGEMANS: How was he after receiving this news?

KELLY: He was really upset. He did not see the gardens at all. He was in a world of his own. He was really quite stressed, very strained, and conversation was extremely difficult.

DINGEMANS: Coming on to Saturday, are you still down in Cornwall?

KELLY: We are indeed. We set off to the Eden Project. It is a huge quarry which has some biospheres in it with tropical and warm temperate plantings within.

DINGEMANS: Did he enjoy seeing it?

KELLY: No. Although it was a lovely World Heritage site, he seemed very grim, very unhappy, extremely tense, but accepting the process he was going through. It was a very grim time for both of us. I have never known him to be as unhappy as he was then.

DINGEMANS: His unhappiness you could feel?

KELLY: It was tangible. Absolutely, palpable.

DINGEMANS: Right. 13th July is a Sunday?

KELLY: That is right. I stayed in Cornwall. David wanted to set off early.

DINGEMANS: Did he go by train or by car?

KELLY: No, he drove by car. I was worried about this. I asked him to drive extremely carefully and to take his time. He was extremely tense. The MoD had offered, by now, to put him up at a hotel in Horse Guards but we all thought especially our daughter Rachel, he would be more comfortable with her. So he set off about 11.30.

DINGEMANS: Did he read anything in the papers that day?

KELLY: Yes, and it did not help. There were other comments about his junior status, about – it was just a total belittling in some ways.

DINGEMANS: What did he think of the belittling of his status as you put it?

KELLY: He was in dismay. I think it was on this day that he said that somebody had told him over the phone while we were down in Cornwall that Jack Straw, who he had supported a few weeks earlier at the Foreign Affairs Committee –

DINGEMANS: I think that was some time in September 2002.

KELLY: Jack Straw had said he was upset at the technical support at that Committee meeting, he had been accompanied by somebody so junior.

DINGEMANS: How had Dr Kelly taken that?

KELLY: He laughed. It was kind of a hysterical laugh in a way. He was deeply, deeply hurt.

DINGEMANS: 15th July we know he goes off to the Foreign Affairs Committee. Did you speak to him at all that day?

KELLY: Later on. This was our 36th wedding anniversary so I was constantly thinking of him all day. He rang that evening and said it had been a total nightmare. Certainly from the television pictures I saw later he really did look very stressed, I could see that.

DINGEMANS: And where does he spend the night on 15th July?

KELLY: At my daughter Rachel's.

DINGEMANS: 16th July we know he goes off to the [Intelligence and Security Committee]. Do you speak to him at all on that day?

KELLY: I spend the day returning from Cornwall by train. I met up with him at Rachel's house.

DINGEMANS: How was he then?

KELLY: He was able to converse a little, but it was very, very strained. He was sort of used up. We made our way home. He did not speak at all during that journey. He was very tense and very, very tired.

DINGEMANS: 17th July is a Thursday. How did he seem?

KELLY: I have no idea. He had never seemed depressed in all of this, but he was very tired and very subdued.

DINGEMANS: Did he have any work to do that day?

KELLY: He said he had a report to write for the MoD. This is the one that somebody on the Foreign Affairs Committee referred to as his 'homework' I think.

DINGEMANS: Some Parliamentary Questions that were tabled?

KELLY: That is right.

DINGEMANS: Do you know whether he made any telephone calls that day?

KELLY: Yes, he was certainly on the phone quite a bit I think. I left the house for a few minutes to meet somebody and pick up some photographs. I came back, went into his study to try and lighten the atmosphere a bit by showing him some photographs and some other data I had got for the History Society. He smiled, stood up and then said he had not quite finished. But a few minutes later he went to sit in the sitting room all by himself without saying anything, which was quite unusual for him, but he went and sat in the sitting room.

DINGEMANS: When was he sitting in the sitting room?

KELLY: From about 12.30 I would think.

DINGEMANS: Did he say anything?

KELLY: No, he just sat and he looked really very tired. By this time I had started with a huge headache and begun to feel sick. In fact I was physically sick several times at this stage because he looked so desperate.

DINGEMANS: Did he have any lunch?

KELLY: He didn't want any lunch he did have some lunch. I made some sandwiches and he had a glass of water. We sat together at the table opposite each other. I tried to make conversation. I was feeling pretty wretched, so was he. He looked distracted and dejected.

DINGEMANS: How would you describe him at this time?

KELLY: Oh, I just thought he had a broken heart. He looked as though he had shrunk, but I had no idea at that stage of what he might do later, absolutely no idea at all. He could not put two sentences together. He could not talk at all. I went to go and have a lie down after lunch, which is something I quite often did just to cope with my arthritis. I said to him, 'What are you going to do?' He said, 'I will probably go for my walk'.

DINGEMANS: What time do you think you went upstairs, so far as you can remember?

KELLY: It would be about half past 1, quarter to 2 perhaps. He went into his study. Then shortly after I had laid down he came to ask me if I was okay. I said: yes, I will be fine. And then he went to change into his jeans and put on his shoes. Then I assumed he had left the house.

DINGEMANS: And did he, in fact, go straight off for his walk?

KELLY: Well, the phone rang a little bit later on and I assumed he had left so I went downstairs to find the telephone in the dining room. By this time the ringing had stopped and I was aware of David talking quietly on a phone. I said something like: I thought you had gone out for a walk. He did not respond of course because he was talking on the phone.

DINGEMANS: Do you know what time this was?

KELLY: Not exactly, no. Getting on for 3, I would think.

DINGEMANS: Do you know who the caller was?

KELLY: I assumed it was the MoD, I am not sure.

DINGEMANS: And did Dr Kelly go out for his walk?

KELLY: He had gone by 3.20.

DINGEMANS: What time did you start to become concerned?

KELLY: Probably late afternoon. Rachel rang, my daughter rang to say: do not worry, he has probably gone out to have a good think. She made a decision to come over. She said: I will go and walk up and meet Dad. She walked up one of the normal footpaths he would have taken. She came back about half an hour or so later.

DINGEMANS: What time was this?

KELLY: This must have been about 6.30 perhaps by now. I am not sure of the times. I was in a terrible state myself by this time trying not to think awful things and trying to take each moment as it came.

DINGEMANS: What was decided to be done?

KELLY: Well, we had delayed calling the police because we thought we might make matters worse if David had returned when we started to search. I felt he was already in a difficult enough situation. So we put off calling the police until about 20 to 12 at night.

DINGEMANS: The police are called. Do they turn up?

KELLY: They turn up. And the search begins.

DINGEMANS: Did you hear any other news?

KELLY: Not initially, no. It was during the morning of the Friday, I think, the 18th by now, that the police came to inform us of David's death.

DINGEMANS: We have heard about the circumstances of Dr Kelly's death and the fact that a knife was used. Were you shown the knife at all?

KELLY: We were not shown the knife. We were shown a photocopy of I presume the knife which we recognised as a knife he had had for many years and kept in his drawer.

DINGEMANS: We have also heard that some co-proxamol was used.

KELLY: Indeed.

DINGEMANS: Do you take any medicine?

KELLY: I do. I take co-proxamol for my arthritis. I keep a small store in a kitchen drawer and the rest in my bedside table.

DINGEMANS: Finally, after Dr Kelly's death there were some reports in the press about him being a Walter Mitty character. What was your reaction to that?

KELLY: I was devastated. That was totally the opposite. He was a very modest, shy, retiring guy. He did not boast at all and he was very factual and that is what he felt his job was. That is what he tried always to be, to be factual.

DINGEMANS: Is there anything else you would like to say?

KELLY: Yes. Lord Hutton, on behalf of my family I would like to thank you and your counsel for the dignified way in which you are carrying out this Inquiry into my husband's death. We would also like to acknowledge the support our family have received from so many people all over the country and elsewhere and, finally, may I take this opportunity to ask the media to continue to respect my family's privacy. We are a very private family. Thank you.

HUTTON: Mrs Kelly, thank you very much indeed.

KELLY: Thank you, my Lord.

HUTTON: I think this will be an appropriate time to adjourn.

USHER: All rise.

For Further Reading

The transcripts of the evidence to the Hutton inquiry and
the documents provided to it by Government departments
are on the inquiry website:
www.the-hutton-inquiry.org.uk

The Commons Foreign Affairs Committee report on the
Decision to go to War in Iraq was published in July 2003,
reference number HC 813-1, ISBN 0 21501162 7 available
from TSO, The Stationery Office email:
book.orders@tso.co.uk

The Parliamentary Intelligence and Security Committee
report on Iraqi Weapons of Mass Destruction – Intelligence
and Assessments, was published in September 2003.
Reference number: Cm 5972, ISBN 0 10 159722 3 available
from TSO (as above).